Judy Freed

STARTS AND FINISHES

STARTS AND FINISHES
COMING OF AGE IN THE FIFTIES

Carey Winfrey

Saturday Review Press | E. P. Dutton & Co., Inc.
New York

A portion of this book appeared in different form in *Harper's* Magazine copyright © 1972 by Carey Winfrey.

LIBRARY OF CONGRESS CATALOGING IN PUBLICATION DATA

Winfrey, Carey.
   Starts and finishes.

   Autobiographical.
   1. Winfrey, Carey. I. Title.
CT275.W58458A34   917.3'03'920924 [B]   74-28086

Copyright © 1975 by Carey Winfrey.
All rights reserved. Printed in the U.S.A.
First Edition

10 9 8 7 6 5 4 3 2 1

No part of this publication may be reproduced or transmitted in any form or by any means, electronic or mechanical, including photocopy, recording, or any information storage and retrieval system now known or to be invented, without permission in writing from the publisher, except by a reviewer who wishes to quote brief passages in connection with a review written for inclusion in a magazine, newspaper, or broadcast.

Published simultaneously in Canada by Clarke, Irwin & Company
Limited, Toronto and Vancouver
ISBN: 0-8415-0371-0

For Laurie

STARTS AND FINISHES

I

My grandfather's biography is engraved on a silver plaque mounted under two thin horseshoes at the National Museum of Racing in Saratoga Springs, New York: "These shoes were worn by Tokalon, winner of the 1906 Brooklyn Handicap. When she came from Texas to win this race she brought with her as groom G. Carey Winfrey, who stayed in the East to become one of New York's greatest trainers." I was named for my grandfather.

In his middle years he was a strong, robust man who loved to arm wrestle and to drive automobiles fast, leaning hard into the steering wheel to make the tires squeal around the turns. He once beat a black groom—broke his jaw with one punch—because he took my father, who was then only nine years old, into the "colored" section of the racetrack cafeteria at the old Empire City track in New York. It wasn't so much what the groom had done as what he said to my grandfather after he did it: "You ain't back in Texas now, Mr. Winfrey." My grandfather *was* from Texas, was a man of his time, and no doubt took a dim view of uppity grooms. But the man I knew as Grandpa never could have hit anyone. Grandpa was not robust. His hands shook from Parkinson's disease. He drove very slowly.

Grandpa smelled like the witch hazel he used in abundance. He was shy and quiet, but he laughed a lot—a big, wide laugh that showed his teeth, with a grin that hung on for a long time after. "How do you and I stand?" he would ask me, at least every day. Properly trained, I would answer, "How *do* we stand, Grandpa?" He would smile then, in happy anticipation of the line he was about to deliver. "On our feet," he'd say. "On our feet." He never got tired of that one, and I never did either.

Unlike my father, who never wagered more than twenty dollars and then only on one of his own horses "for luck," my grandfather enjoyed making a hefty bet every now and then. He once bet five hundred dollars on one of his own colts. The colt went off at twelve to one; my grandmother used to tell about that afternoon when my grandfather came home with a suitcase, opened it, and covered the bed with six thousand dollars in green paper bills.

It may have been the occasional wager that took my grandfather to the races every day, but I don't think so. He just loved racing. Most of his humor involved some kind of play on the racetrack life. Whenever he saw a pretty girl walking by, he would pull out his stopwatch as if he were clocking her. "Eighteen and two," he might say, admiringly. If she were wearing high heels, he might shake his head. "You know, if I was trainin' that filly," he'd say to me, "I'd clip her heels a little."

Whenever anybody would ask who this or that horse was "by"—meaning who the sire was—my grandfather would wink at me. "He was by *himself* the last time I looked," he would say with his big grin.

He could remember a race at Bowie in "nineteen and nine" as if he had seen it that morning. Most of his stories dated from the old days, like the time Blue Steel, a groom, came to work late one morning. The groom explained that he'd been thrown off the streetcar and had had to walk to work. My grandfather asked why he'd been thrown off. Well, Blue Steel explained, he had gotten on and walked to the back of the streetcar just as he always did. Yes, said my grandfather. Then, Blue Steel said, this other colored fellow got on the streetcar. Yes, said my grandfather. Then, said Blue Steel, this colored fella set right up front with the white folk. "Well naturally," said Blue Steel, "I went up and sat in the front too. Just cause this nigger wore a turban didn't make him no better than me." The conductor told Blue Steel he would have to go to the back of the car. Blue Steel protested. "What about this fellow next to me?" he asked. "He's just as black as I am."

"But he's Hindu," the conductor said to Blue Steel. Blue Steel looked at the conductor. The only Hindoo he knew was a three-year-old colt who had won his last four races. "If he's Hindoo," he said at last, "then I'm Man O'War."

My grandfather could remember a hundred such stories. But he had difficulty with the more recent past. He always called me "Bill, uh, Carey," seeing my father as a child so clearly in me. Or he would ask me to turn up the "radio" when he meant the television. Right before he died, he took to calling it the "piano."

His poor memory bothered him a great deal. What upset him most was forgetting the names of the horses he trained. To combat this deficiency, he kept a small notebook with the horses' names listed on separate pages, in just the order they stood in their stalls in the shed. The idea was that he could walk along, turning one page for each stall, and always know the name of the horse in front of him. The only problem with the system was that he kept losing the book.

My grandfather was never as famous a trainer as my father would be. Other horsemen knew how good he was, however, and the smart bettor did too. He wintered his horses in New York instead of taking them to race in California or Florida as most trainers did. When racing returned to New York in the spring, my grandfather's horses would be rested, used to the weather, used to the racetrack, and in peak form. In the spring of 1955 he saddled ten winners out of his first sixteen starters. That fall the New York Turf Writers' Association voted him Trainer of the Year.

When my grandfather heard about the award he couldn't believe it. "They must mean Bill," he said. Finally, convinced they indeed meant him, he developed elaborate fears about the presentation ceremonies. "Sunny Jim" Fitzsimmons, then eighty-two, took him aside. "Now, son," he said to my seventy-one-year-old grandfather, "don't get excited. Just take it easy as if you are saddling an old plater for an overnight race."

"But what will I say when he hands me the plaque?" my grandfather asked.

"Just say thanks," said Mr. Fitz. Which is just what my grandfather did.

My father won his first horse race as a boy of nine, riding a circus pony named Sparkle at the old Jamaica track on Long Island. I don't know how many other horses there were in the race, but my grandfather once told me that the others were under considerable restraint. In the picture taken in the winner's circle, my father's face is ceremonially serious, but the men standing around in black suits and hats behind him are all smiles.

He was seventeen when he won his second race, this time as a jockey in real competition. "Congratulations," my grandfather said to my grandmother in a telegram. "Bill won his first race today." A yellowed newspaper clipping in my grandmother's scrapbook is more detailed: "Willie Winfrey rode his first winner here this afternoon. Son of G. Carey Winfrey, well-known owner and trainer, Willie has been trying to crash the winner's circle since early in the last Florida campaign. . . . Eight answered the call, but little Willie showed them the way home. He brought the BB Stable's two-year-old from behind in a rattling stretch drive to take command in the closing strides. The stable gang gave the little boy a great big hand.''

Rattling stretch drives and stable gangs' applause notwithstanding, my father is convinced that the greatest mistake he made in life was quitting school in the ninth grade to become a jockey. He blamed his parents for letting him do it. He would never make the same mistake with me.

My father's riding career lasted less than a year. He put on too much weight and became, at eighteen, the youngest licensed horse trainer in the country, taking a string of horses from my grandfather's stable up to Canada.

By 1941, the year Whirlaway won the Triple Crown and the year I was born, my father had a new car, a savings account, a growing reputation, and a terrific filly named Dini, who was winning everything in sight.

I was asleep in my crib, a week more than four months old, and my father was on the golf course, when the news of the attack on Pearl Harbor came over the radio. We were in Miami, where my father had brought my mother and me and a stable full of horses the month before from Long Island.

The timing was unfortunate for my father. He had begun to make a real name for himself on the racetrack, and was not anxious to abandon a blossoming career. Or us, either, for that matter. He and my mother had been married less than two years. I was very appealing at four months. The timing was bad.

For a while it looked very much as if he would join the Coast Guard, following other horsemen who had been enticed by the prospect of a commission and work with horses in something called the Coast Patrol. Coast Patrollers rode horses up and down the eastern coast of Florida, on the lookout for German submarines. Although no Coast Patroller was ever known to have actually spotted a submarine, German or otherwise, one of my father's horse-training friends spent the better part of a moonless night holding a German U-boat captain at bay with his rifle near Vero Beach.

"If you move so much as a hair on your head," my father's friend shouted, "I'll shoot it off." The U-boat captain did not move a muscle. Indeed, when dawn broke several hours later the captain had unaccountably metamorphosed into a fencepost.

A racetrack official told my father that he could arrange a commission for him in the Coast Patrol. But during his physical examination my father was discovered to have a cyst, ignominiously located in the crack of his buttocks. He was turned down cold.

In the spring of 1942 the three of us, and the horses, returned to New York. There my father had his cyst removed and began sitting out the war on a rubber innertube.

In Miami the following winter he reported again to his draft board, ready to serve his country. But the lady behind the desk, perhaps envisioning a fatherless young boy, violated her professional ethics by pointing out to my father that if he were to go to work for, say, an airline, she and her fellow draft boarders would be powerless to touch him. My father thought this over and shortly found himself driving from the racetrack each morning to the Miami airport to unload planes for Eastern Airlines. It was hot work and the hours were long, particularly after mornings that had begun at five. But the work wasn't what bothered him. What began to gnaw on him was the feeling that he was ducking the war in a way that was unworthy of him. So he said the hell with it and joined the Marines.

While my father earned his stripe at boot camp, my mother did some shaping up too, enrolling in a program called Ann Delafield's Success Course. It was, in fact, a high-priced gym class. My mother lost twenty-two pounds. She remembers with no small suggestion of pride that even though she counted "a senator's wife, a debutante, a champion swimmer, and at least two models" among her classmates, it was she who was chosen to represent the "school" in an advertisement. She was told she had an "interesting face." The ad was going to play on the idea of the marine's wife getting in shape for her husband. The photographer came. The ad was set in type. At the last moment Ann Delafield changed her mind and stopped the ad. Too many soldiers weren't coming back.

My mother also spent time having lunch with my father's mother in fashionable Manhattan restaurants. It was at one such lunch, after only a couple of martinis, that they decided that what my father needed most, what with summer coming on, were some lightweight, cool uniforms. The salesman at Brooks Brothers was most accommodating. He showed them the catalog and turned to the page marked "United States Marine Corps, Summer Service Alpha." My mother and grandmother gave the salesman my father's size and measurements and ordered three complete sets, tailor-made.

When my father finished boot camp at Parris Island, South Carolina, and came to New York on leave, he was very pleased with his new uniforms; at boot camp he had worn nothing but fatigues. With only one visit to the Brooks Brothers tailor, they fit perfectly.

The first time he put them on was the day he drove back to Parris Island, where he had received orders to stay on as a rifle instructor for the recruits coming along behind him. My mother was going with him to check out the dependents' quarters. They drove as far as Petersburg, Virginia, the first day and checked into a hotel.

They must have been a splendid-looking couple that evening, my mother beautiful in a smart new summer outfit, my father fit and tanned in his new uniform. They found a restaurant and had a couple of drinks and a good dinner. It was only on the way back to the hotel that my father began to suspect that something was the matter. The waiter's calling him "sir" hadn't seemed so unusual. Lots of waiters in lots of restaurants had called him "sir."

They hadn't walked more than a hundred yards or so from the restaurant when it first happened.

"Yes, dammit," my father said to my mother. "I *am* sure. They *saluted* me."

Another group of soldiers walked toward them. "Good evening, sir," they chorused, their hands coming smartly to their cap brims.

With his eyes on the ground near his feet, my father brought his hand above his eyes. "Uh, good evening," he muttered.

To my mother he whispered, "Let's get the hell outta here."

My mother already knew that somehow the uniform was to blame. But she had no idea just why or how. As for the epaulets on the shoulders, she thought them "distinctive." A little extra bit of flair. It had no more occurred to her that the man at Brooks Brothers would not know my father wasn't an officer than it would have occurred to the salesman that these two charming women would order tailor-made uniforms for a boot recruit.

My mother had grown up, pretty and poor, in Brockton, Massachusetts, which was known for men's shoes before it was known as the hometown of Rocky Marciano, who in 1952 knocked out Jersey Joe Walcott to become the heavyweight boxing champion of the world.

She was a very young girl when her father packed up and left one morning. Right after high school my mother deserted Brockton too, taking a Greyhound bus to New York City. She brought with her one small suitcase and a dazzling smile, which helped her land a job with Best & Company, modeling those square-shouldered dresses and thick-soled shoes that were fashionable in the mid-1930s. After about a year in New York she was sent to the store's new branch in Miami

Beach. Not long after her arrival she was photographed running out of the surf. The caption, as it appeared in the New York *Daily Mirror* of January 18, 1936, noted: "A typical bathing beauty after an invigorating dip in the pleasant Atlantic."

It was on that same beach, about a year later, that she met my father, who had come to Florida to race his horses. Neither of them had had a great deal of experience with the opposite sex—or with the world at large, for that matter—and in a short time, they took each other for better or for worse. They were married in 1939.

Their first few years together were dazzling. The young up-and-coming trainer with the pretty wife was much in demand. They went to parties; they got the best tables at restaurants and nightclubs in Miami, New Orleans, New York, and Saratoga. They took fishing trips to Havana and had ringside tickets to the fights at Madison Square Garden. For my mother there were sequined dresses, new cars, a mink coat, and a house in Miami.

Parris Island came as an enormous shock to her. She was unprepared for the tiny, dirty room with the toilet down the hall that the United States Marine Corps deemed appropriate for the wives and children of privates first class. She took it personally that she was not allowed in the officers' club. She found the enlisted men's club loud and rowdy. After two days she returned to New York to await word from my father that he had found suitable accommodations.

But my father had little time for house hunting. Each morning he was on the rifle range by five, kneeling next to some recruit, showing him how to "breathe . . . relax . . . s-q-u-e-e-z-e" the trigger, ever so slowly. (Later, after the war, my father would chant the litany of the rifle range while I listened, entranced: "Rrrready on the left . . . rrrready on the right . . . alllllll ready on the firing line." When I heard that chant again years later, as a Marine officer candidate on a rifle range at Quantico, Virginia, it seemed to lack my father's rolling resonances. But of course no drill instructor could have measured up to two decades of anticipation.)

My father finally sent word that the best he could come up with was a boarding house in Beaufort, South Carolina. My mother and I could stay there while she looked around for something better.

The room my father had found for us was on the top floor of a three-story walkup. My mother arrived with enough baggage to last the winter. It took her three trips to get it all upstairs; the other denizens simply gazed upon her with looks compounded of lassitude and contempt. Apparently they had decided we were either Yankees or Marine dependents, possibly even both, and in either case not worth lending a hand to.

Hot, tired, and dirty, my mother wanted nothing more than to shower and wash her hair. But the little bath down the hall had no shower, only a rusty tub. Carrying me in her arms, she sought out the nearest drugstore, in search of a rubber spray attachment that would convert the tub into something akin to a shower. The druggist eyed her suspiciously. Yes, he had such an attachment, but what did she want to use it for? My mother told him, took it, and paid for it. She asked him if she could return it if it didn't fit. "Nope," the druggist said simply. My mother then suggested to the druggist another use for his rubber hose.

My father came to the boarding house the first thing the next morning. My mother told him she was very sorry, she wanted to be with him, but she had me to consider. She would not stay in a town that was still fighting the Civil War. We left for Miami the next day.

In the fall of 1943 Paul Robeson opened to exultant notices on Broadway for his performance as Othello. Sid Luckman completed sixty-two out of a hundred passes for the Chicago Bears. Errol Flynn appeared on the screen as an anti-Nazi Royal Canadian Mountie and Technical Sergeant Gerald L. Smith was revealed as the author of the one millionth fan letter received by Miss Rita Hayworth (which entitled him to a day on the set with the object of his affection). Drew Pearson revealed that in a tent hospital in Sicily, General George ("Blood and Guts") Patton had slapped a shell-shocked soldier, calling him "yellow-bellied." Roosevelt, Churchill, and Stalin conferred at Teheran, and *Look* magazine paid the sum of two thousand dollars for a photograph of Mrs. Roosevelt on a trip to Africa rubbing noses with a Maori tribeswoman. There were 7.7 million men in uniform but Frank ("The Voice") Sinatra was not among them. Three days before his twenty-sixth birthday the singer was classified 4-F by the Newark induction center because of a punctured eardrum. Fats Waller died on a train in Kansas City at the age of thirty-nine and on a Pacific island called Tarawa the United States Marines suffered more than thirty-five hundred casualties in six hours. As fall gave way to winter, a lot of young marines found themselves with sets of orders they had not expected. My father was one of them. After ten days on leave with us in Miami, my father went overseas to war on Christmas Day, 1943.

He left my mother distraught. She cried and she pouted. For a week she refused even to leave the house. Her friends told her she was being silly. Even my father's parents urged her to go out.

At about eleven o'clock on New Year's Eve my mother's girlfriend Beverly called her on the telephone. In the background my mother could hear people laughing and the clink of glasses. Beverly said to stop being so dramatic and come on over. My mother said okay, she would. She arrived to find a house full of young paratroopers and sailors and soldiers and a lot of pretty girls like herself. She doesn't remember the man who offered her a drink. She does remember the man who came up behind her and told her not to take it.

"That's rot gut," said the second man, pulling out a flask. "Here, have a real drink."

His name was Dick Evans. Dick Evans was a fat man with

a red face and a laugh like a machine gun. He slicked his hair straight back and ran a gambling casino called the Little Palm Club. The specialty of the house was half an avocado filled with fresh shrimp. Ann Sheridan was a regular. So, in time, was my mother.

My mother saw a lot of the Little Palm Club and a lot of Dick Evans while my father was overseas. Dick Evans was much older than she was. He liked to show her off to his friends and to take her places. My mother liked not being lonely and laughing at the stories Dick Evans told about being a gambler and a drinker during prohibition.

He taught her things. He taught her about good food and good conversation and lively parties and being "social." She learned to smoke without coughing and to drink without falling down, to stay up "to all hours," and to make men laugh.

My father had been learning different things. He had learned to carry a field-marching pack over miles of jungle trails without touching his canteen. He learned to dig foxholes with a small folding shovel called an entrenching tool and to roll his tent up in the dark. And he learned how to skindive with goggles made by the natives on the islands of Truk and Guam. It was while on Truk that my father rescued a drowned man. Or, more correctly, he *retrieved* him.

My father doesn't remember how it happened that they discovered Baxter missing. One moment Baxter was swimming and roughhousing with the rest of them. The next moment he had disappeared. The lieutenant called on my father to look for him. The reason my father was chosen, he was careful to explain to me later, was because he did not smoke cigarettes. He took a great breath and dived into the water at the place where Baxter had last been seen. It was about twenty feet deep.

There was no sign of Baxter. My father swam in an ever-expanding circle. A minute passed, then half of the next. Spent, he headed for the surface. Looking back one last time, he saw something. He grabbed Baxter by the hair and pulled him toward the surface. He wondered if he would black out before reaching fresh air.

While my father lay on his back getting his breath, the lieutenant gave Baxter artificial respiration. Baxter never moved, never even coughed.

The drowned man episode was as close as my father came to being a war hero. Of course the story is flawed by the death of the man, a fine point that never occurred to me the many times I begged my father to recount the adventure after he came back from the war in 1945. It was years later before I realized that my father had told the story as a kind of parable of the clean life: my father had been *chosen* because he didn't smoke. I simply thought it the purest act of courage the world had ever known.

My father didn't see much fighting. A few Japanese on Guam who didn't know the war was lost fired an occasional round in his general direction. And he stood guard plenty of times over scrawny Japanese prisoners herded into a chickenwire enclosure at Truk. But no real action. He had grown a mustache and shaved it off. He had used foul language and then decided against it. He even took up smoking for a while before swearing off it for good. What my father brought back from the war was a Japanese pistol, a Japanese sword, and an older, more settled version of himself.

The story is told that the night my father arrived home in Miami, discharged at last, he kissed my mother and held her in his arms and said how wonderful it was to be back home again. He picked me up over his head and laughed and told me how big I'd gotten while he was away, so big he could scarcely recognize me (a problem I shared to an even greater extent regarding him). Then he made himself a drink, loosened his tie, sat down on the couch, and stretched his feet onto the coffee table.

"Take your feet," my mother is supposed to have said, "off my coffee table."

My mother says it isn't true. She says she probably did worse things—but she doesn't remember anything about any coffee table.

What she does remember about that first night home is that my father wanted spaghetti, a request she found faintly repugnant. Dutifully, however, she put water on to boil and opened a can of tomato sauce.

"Ah," said my father when he was served. "Delicious. Now the only thing I could use would be Parmesan cheese."

"Parmesan cheese!" my mother recalls saying. "He wants Parmesan cheese," she added to no one in particular. "I suppose they gave you Parmesan cheese in the Marine Corps too?"

I was too young to remember such conversations. But a saying of my mother's that I do remember and that probably dates to this period was "Eat it or wear it." My mother used to say that to my father if he happened to look less than joyous when she served him dinner. No matter how many times she had said it to him before, each time she said "Eat it or wear it" she always indicated with a particular look that she thought it an unusually clever and original thing to say.

Yet it is my mother, more than anyone, who has painted the picture I have of my father as long-suffering. He never talks about those days. It was my mother, for example, who told me about the time my father took the phone call about Dick Evans right after the war. It was a coroner calling from New York to tell my mother that Dick Evans had dropped dead at the Waldorf-Astoria. He had died, the coroner said, reaching for a piece of chocolate candy. They had found my mother's name in his address book. Though my father had never heard of Dick Evans and must have given some thought to what his wife's name was doing in his address book, he told the coroner that my mother was out and that he would pass the information along to her. Which he did, never even asking her who is this Dick Evans anyway. Later my mother learned that Dick Evans had died of a heart attack. He had come to New York to see a heart specialist; his appointment was for the following morning.

Certainly my mother and father had married too young, with too little experience behind them. And just as they had begun to grow up together they had been separated and had lived vastly different lives for the better part of two years. When my father finally returned, he faced high mortgage payments and an indifferent reception at the racetrack. It was only natural that there would be problems. Yet at the center of my parents' difficulties lay, of all things, me.

I was two when he left, four when he came back. My mother had used those two years to establish absolute charge over me. She had bathed me and fed me, made my clothes, and made me giggle. She was not about to turn over one bit of her authority to any newly returned stranger, even though his name was Daddy.

My mother's idea of child raising was based on the pleasure principle. Make me happy. Keep me smiling. Straighten my room. Buy me toys. If I wanted it, serve me French toast every morning with Vermont Maid syrup. And if I did not like plain, white, cow's milk, let me have chocolate milk.

"Chocolate milk!" My father, who had lived on C-rations for weeks at a time and was proud of it, was aghast. Tell him I was out stealing hubcaps. Tell him I had played doctor with the little girl across the street. Tell him I had driven his car into a palm tree. But don't tell him I wanted chocolate milk. Not at breakfast.

In a way the chocolate milk argument—a silly, unproductive barrage that nobody won—seemed to symbolize all that had gone wrong between them. The more outraged at my pampered behavior my father got, the more my mother sought to make life easier for me. The more she softened my path, the more he sought to toughen it. (The pattern, thus established, was to last for more than a decade. In years to come he contrived summer jobs for me away from what he considered the protective atmosphere created by my mother. He sent me to a military boarding school, the deprivations of which so offended my mother that on vacations she spoiled me to extravagance, creating a kind of geographically induced schizophrenia.)

My mother became more openly affectionate; my father increasingly hid his love behind a stern façade. He fervently believed that I needed toughness more than anything else and that if he didn't provide it, no one would. Though he was probably right, I always felt it a loss for us both that he was unable for so many years to stop thinking of me as a boy who would willingly desecrate nature's perfect drink with a dash of Hershey's chocolate syrup.

After the war my parents' lives, together or apart, were dictated by racing schedules: spring, summer, and fall in New York at Aqueduct, Belmont, Jamaica, and Saratoga; the winter months—November through March—in Florida at Hialeah, Gulfstream, and Tropical Park.

My father had been back training horses only a couple of years when my entrance into the first grade forced him to face the problem of mobility. Was I to be enrolled in school in New York, only to leave after a couple of months to go to Florida, then to return again to New York to finish out the school year? My mother was adamant. Her son, she declared without possibility of discussion, would not become a vagabond. She would take me to Florida in September to put me in school; my father could join us in November. Moreover, she would stay with me in Florida when my father returned to New York in March. The idea of my boarding at school, she said, was out of the question. That such a schedule would keep them separated six months out of the year was just too bad.

It was about this same time, as it happened, that my father found himself training his first good horse since before the war, a filly named Sweet Dream. Sweet Dream won a number of small stakes races that year (with handsome purses of which my father collected 10 percent). Consequently, his intention to send me to the local public school was, with my mother's urging, upgraded in favor of Miami Country Day and Resident School for Boys.

Country Day was one of those WASP havens based loosely on the English public school. That it was somehow superior, and that by extension those of us who wore its crested T-shirts were also, we took for granted; "the deserved edge" is what our gnarled headmaster said we were acquiring. It was elitist, antidemocratic, permissive, protective, almost assuredly discriminatory. From my first day there I loved it.

I loved Mr. Ellis, who picked me up each morning in an old airport limousine that looked like a 1946 DeSoto except that it had six back seats and was therefore twenty feet long. Mr. Ellis taught history, read Lee's *Lieutenants,* visited Civil War battlegrounds during summer vacations, bemoaned the Philadelphia Phillies, maintained a rapt school bus with stories invented in passing, and dubbed me "Winnie Carefree." My first day of school I learned Mr. Ellis's name and how to arrange my fingers in that rough approximation of the male genitalia that served as our universal riposte for years before we understood its meaning.

I am seven or eight years old and deep asleep in the still hour before dawn. In a little while my father will come and sit on the edge of my bed, rubbing my back slow and warm to wake me.

But now I am dreaming: I am watching Les or John or one of the other grooms braid the tail of a gleaming chestnut thoroughbred colt, beautifying him before a race. I am sitting cross-legged at the door of the stall, listening to the whispery soft psssss-psssss sound the groom makes, exhaling, to keep the horsehairs from getting in his mouth. Then my father appears. He is upset.

"The jock can't ride," he announces to no one in particular. "We'll have to scratch."

Now the dream gets hazy. But somehow, in a moment, miraculously, I am splendidly anointed in racing silks, the whip in my right hand, the stirrups pulled so high my hands are cradled by my knees. The dream is clear again: we are led into the starting gate. I hear my heart tharumping in my chest.

"No chance!" I yell to the starter on his platform. "No chance, Mr. Cassidy!" My horse is still. The bell rings, the doors fly open, and with a lurch that all but throws me from the saddle we are off. I hit the colt three times with my whip, each timed to his stride—bam, pause; bam, pause; bam—just to get him going. Now I sit back, holding him in, saving his speed, rating him, riding easy down the backstretch. Rounding the last turn, heading for home, I start to make my move. Now I hear a murmuring in the grandstand. It grows, as I pass horses, into a roar. I am whipping again, now on the half-stride—bam, bam, bam, bam—still passing horses, the colt and I moving as one. There is but one horse and rider in front of me. Creeping up on them, I am perilously close to waking, twisting in the sheets from excitement. It is all I can do to hang on for my inevitable, but still miraculous . . . VICTORY BY A NOSE!

Of all the dreams of all the things I would have liked to be, my jockey dream was the most constant, the most satisfying, and the most sincere.

We would get up those mornings about 5:30, my father and I, splashing cold water on our faces, moving quietly through the house so as not to wake my mother. The streetlights would be haloed in the morning dew as we drove through half-deserted streets, the radio blaring Jo Stafford or Frankie Laine and "Mule Traaaaaaaaaiiiiiin . . . clippety cloppin' over hill and plain . . ."

Although my father owned lots of automobiles, the one I remember best was a bright red jeepster with rattly plastic side curtains that passed for windows. We would bounce along, the curtains flapping in the wind, the two of us singing to the radio, in tune only with each other. On such mornings I would lean against my father's warmth and never suspect there was any other thing to be but happy.

Dawn would be breaking as we drove up to the stable. The first "set" of horses, half a dozen or so, would already be saddled. Seeing us arrive, the exercise boys would gulp the last swallows of their coffee and get ready to mount their horses. I would walk down the long shed past the horses in their stalls, twenty or more. It was a ritual my father insisted on—saying good morning to the grooms and exercise boys who worked for him. "Good morning, Apples." "Good morning, Harold."

Once the exercise boys had mounted, they would walk their horses to the training track, while I would follow my father on foot to the clocking stand, stopping along the way as he exchanged cheery small talk ("You know my boy Carey") with the other trainers. Even though I never managed to decipher it, I enjoyed the cryptic language of the clockers: "Twenty-two and two for the bay colt. Wha'dju gettim in, Jack?"

By the time my father and I had made our way back to the stable, the grooms would have unsaddled the horses and would have begun to wash them down. The exercise boys, holding the shanks of their steaming mounts, reviewed the workout: "We break at the quarter pole real good. Then my filly, she see a bird or something so she break stride . . ." The horses, frisky now, would shift from side to side, tugging the exercise boys to their tiptoes and kicking out with their hind legs as the grooms ("Hey now, poppa, wha'sa matter wit chu?") lavished steaming buckets of pine-solvented water on the sweating bodies, slopping it on in melon-sized ocean sponges before whisking their hides gleaming dry with long aluminum scrapers. Often, after the horses were bathed, my father would tell me to take the shank of a quieter colt or filly and I would join the parade around the cooling-out ring.

The climax of the morning came when it was time for me to ride the "pony," a name applied to any nonthoroughbred on the track, usually a quarter horse or polo horse. For as long as I can remember my father's pony was named Bill. I don't know how many "Pony Bills" we had in the years I spent my weekends and summers at the track, but I think I must have fallen off every one of them. Even if I was hurt, as I was a couple of times, my father would always make me get right back on and ride some more. Otherwise, he said, it would be much harder the next time. Scared, crying, I might protest that I couldn't hold him, that he'd run away with me again. My father would ignore my plea, his logic incontrovertible: "You can ride as fast as he can run." And back up I'd go while Apples or Harold or Ernie would laugh out loud.

The worst time—I must have been about six—was when an all-brown refugee from the polo fields, Pony Bill the Fourth I think he was, ran away with me at the finish line at Hialeah, galloping all the way back to the stable while I clung to his neck, my feet dangling from the stirrups. Apples was the one to grab him. Pony Bill stopped so fast that I fell right on the ground, just at Apples's feet. He never let me forget about it. I know that if I were to see him tomorrow, he'd ask about "that time at Hialeah" and start to laugh.

Painful though it was, my father's perseverance paid off. By the time I was dreaming my recurring jockey dream, I had learned to ride with confidence if not with style. It was along about this time too that the chain of ex-polo Pony Bills gave way to an exquisite quarter horse named Rusty. The color of an Irish setter, with a mane as long as Godiva's hair, Rusty was as fast—over a quarter of a mile—as any thoroughbred in the barn. He loved nothing better than to open up full throttle, while I, in idolatrous imitation of Arcaro,

Atkinson, and Shoemaker, rode high in the saddle, the stirrups as short as I could make them.

We'd start off slow, galloping easy in the middle of the track. To the untrained eye, we looked like a real racehorse and a real exercise boy. I suspect Rusty enjoyed the role as much as I did. With my head so close to his I could whisper in his ear, and with my fanny far above my head, I would cluck and nudge him in the ribs with my boots. We'd edge in closer to the rail, Rusty reaching out faster and faster, until, at the head of the stretch and heading for home, Rusty would be *racing*. His mane would lash my face, making rivulets of tears, and in my ears the wind was like a cheering throng.

II

Both my mother and father would say in retrospect that they just hadn't had anything in common. But that wasn't strictly so. They both had a sinus condition.

My father's took the form of phlegm in the throat. Perhaps a dozen times on the way to the stable early in the morning, he would roll the car window down, clear his throat, spit, and roll the window up again all in one smooth motion. (Riding beside him, I thought spitting in that way an act of maturity, in roughly the same category as shaving.)

My mother's sinus condition came on suddenly after a cold on a fishing trip in the Florida Keys with my father and another couple. My father told her the best thing for the pain she began to feel behind her nose was a good snoutful of salt water, which she immediately inhaled. Naturally that was just about the worst thing. Soon the pain was so bad they had to cut the fishing trip short and return to Miami. My father had her call his doctor for an appointment. He was booked up solid. But, she was told, he did have a partner. That's how she met Larry.

Larry drained her sinuses and packed her nose with cotton. He told her the packing should be removed in a week's time. As my father would be back in New York by then, my mother was concerned. "Do you mean I have to take it out by myself?" she asked.

"Well, yes, I suppose so," said the doctor. "That is . . . well, where do you live?"

"Miami Shores," my mother said.

"Oh," said the doctor. "Well, then, that's very near me. I can stop by on my way home from work."

When my mother introduced him to me, I asked if he was the father of my second-grade classmate with the same name. He said he was, and when he finished removing the cotton packing my mother asked him if he would like a drink. He confessed that he would like one very much. When he finished his drink, and a second, he suggested that, since they were both single parents, however temporarily, it might be nice some evening to take the boys out to dinner. My mother agreed that it just might be. Even in those days when a house call was not such a rarity, I knew something was up. My verdict was thumbs down.

But where I saw a pompous poseur, my mother saw intelligence and respectability. Where I saw humorlessness, my mother saw poise.

Larry had seen a lot of action during the war, my mother told me, treating the wounded on the front lines in Italy. His temples, she said, had turned gray overnight during one of the bad shellings. If he seemed a bit serious, well, he had his reasons.

By the time my mother joined my father in New York in the summer of 1949, she was convinced she was in love with Larry. Living with my father in a small apartment without air-conditioning through a hot summer did little to change her mind. She could hardly wait to take me back to Miami in the fall. Larry was there to meet the train.

When my father joined us in November, my mother told

him she was seeing another man. For a while my father took to sleeping in a little room at the barn at Hialeah racetrack. I'd see him on the weekends; he'd take me to the beach.

I loved to go to the beach with my father. We'd play tag in the water. We'd race each other. He'd try to teach me to float on my back. We'd throw a football or join a volleyball game, and then eat hot dogs and drink "black cows"—root beer and ice cream.

He'd let me hit his arm, just below the shoulder, as hard as I could with my fist, as if it were a punching bag.

"Oooooh," he'd moan, pretending I had hurt him. Then he'd pick me up, run to the water, and throw me into a wave.

"Daddy," I'd say, maybe thirty times in an afternoon.

"Whatty?" he'd answer.

Most of the time I didn't have a question. I just liked to hear him answer.

For a while it was just the two of us. Then he found a new beach buddy. Her name was Jane. Jane was a tomboy, who had grown up good-looking in a healthy outdoor way. She laughed a lot, sort of hearty like a man.

I was crazy about her. And I hated her. I hated her for making my father laugh when my mother couldn't or wouldn't. I loved her for the same reason. And of course I hated sharing him with her.

Though she teased me for being whiny and sometimes sent me off to play by myself, I liked Jane okay when we were at the beach. It was the trip home I didn't like.

Our route took us by a little bar on Biscayne Boulevard that had a table shuffleboard. We always stopped there. I thought it was one thing for Jane to go to the beach with my father, but quite another for her to drink beer and play shuffleboard with him. I bought a nickel notebook into which I recorded the date and the number of beers Jane and my father drank on the way from the beach.

For a long time my father had promised to take me and my

cousin Judy to the circus. I had built the thing up in my mind to a huge event—it *was* Ringling Brothers and Barnum & Bailey after all—and when the day finally rolled around I was practically apoplectic with excitement.

Dutifully my father and Jane took Judy and me to the animal cages beforehand. We tried to cheer up Gargantua, the famous gorilla, who was sick that day. They bought us peanuts and cotton candy. Then we took our seats under the big top. The show had scarcely started when Jane said she had to go to the bathroom.

"That's funny," my father said. "I do too." They said that they would be right back.

They were gone for three hours. They missed everything. The lions. The clowns. The horses. The seals. They even missed the Flying Wallendas. There was so much I wanted my father to have seen with me. So much he could have told me about the various acts. People had already started filing out of the tent and the circus people had started putting canvas over their equipment when my father and Jane finally got back to us. They had been drinking. They had bought circus hats and each of them carried a souvenir lion tamer's whip. They pretended to have seen it all. "Whooo, whee, some show," said my father. Jane laughed.

I was feverish with anger. The drive home was awful. My father and Jane whooped and laughed and beat the side of the car with their whips, pretending they were jockeys in a race. I crawled down on the floor of the back seat and put my hands over my ears.

I'm sure I must have seen Jane again. There may even have been more times at the beach. But I don't remember her from that night on.

My father decided that what had gone wrong with their marriage came from living in Miami and being separated all those months each year. He persuaded my mother to try life in New York. When racing moved back there in March of 1950, he went north with the idea of finding a house for the three of us.

My father had been back in New York only a week when he got a phone call from Jane. She told him that my mother was seeing Larry again. My father flew to Florida and confronted my mother. She said she was sorry, that yes she did want to save the marriage. She said she wouldn't see Larry any more.

When my father got back to New York he telephoned Jane. He told her that my mother and he had decided to try to patch things up. He wouldn't be seeing her again.

It was about an hour later that Jane called my father's sister, my aunt. Her voice was thick and slow; my aunt made out the words "pills" and the phrase "so sorry for the trouble." My aunt called my mother and told her about Jane's call.

They drove to Jane's house. Jane was asleep on the living room floor. In the bathroom they found an empty vial of sleeping pills. My mother stuck her finger down Jane's throat to make her throw up. When she started to come to, they walked her to the car and drove to my mother's friend's house, where they led Jane fully clothed into the swimming pool. The cold water brought her around.

About two weeks later we left for Long Island and a new life in the country.

The house we moved into was surrounded by woods and streams, snakes and tadpoles, rabbits and woodchucks. My father gave me the choice of having a BB gun that would be mine to use anytime I wanted, or a .22 that we would shoot only together. I chose the BB gun.

The house had once been the barn of a great estate. The living room went straight up three floors to a ceiling forty feet off the ground with a huge fireplace in the center.

The only bad thing about the house was its acoustics. The

high peaked ceiling reflected the sounds of the violent arguments my mother and father were soon having. My mother would get nearly hysterical, sometimes screaming at my father at the top of her lungs.

The year 1950 was a big one for my father. He trained three terrific horses—a colt named Loser Weeper and two fillies, Bed O'Roses and Next Move. The three of them had been winning a lot of the kind of races that were just starting to be televised. If I didn't go to the races, I'd watch them on television. If he won, my father would be interviewed after the race. He was always very businesslike in those interviews, in what was to me frustrating contrast to Eric Guerin, the regular jockey. Whenever Guerin was interviewed, he would always say hello to his son first thing. "Hi Ronnie," he would say. Sometimes he'd say "Hi Ronnie" again between the different questions the interviewer asked him: "Hi Ronnie, hi Ronnie." My father, however, stuck strictly to the subject at hand. I had pleaded with him to say hello to me on television but he always said he couldn't do that.

The Suburban Handicap was a particularly important race for my father and for Loser Weeper. It carried with it a purse of fifty thousand dollars, an enormous sum in racing in 1950, and it was generally regarded as the championship test for four-year-olds in the same way that the Belmont (and not the Derby, whose history and tradition capture the public fancy) is the great test for three-year-olds.

I watched the Suburban with two brothers who lived near us. It was a splendid race, with Loser Weeper coming up strong on the outside to win by more than a length. I was jubilant, and obviously my father was too. I could see him on television laughing with Alfred Vanderbilt, the owner, and with Eric Guerin. I could see him patting Loser Weeper on the neck with great affection. The interviewer came up to him, sticking the microphone in his face. But before he could ask a question, my father, shaking his head and sort of laughing to himself, began to speak. "Before anything else," he said, "I've got to say hello to my boy Carey or else he won't speak to me when I get home."

"Whoopieeee," I whooped. I never heard what my father said after that because the three of us were out of the room, bursting with energy and excitement. We got on our bicycles. We rode out on the road, heading for a hill that led down under the railroad bridge. Suddenly we were racing. I was on Loser Weeper, streaking furiously down the hill. In the Loser Weeper manner, I was sweeping by my adversaries on the outside when the thin wheel of my English bicycle hit a stone, or lodged in a rut, or somehow buckled. I was thrown over it, landing, as my father put it afterward, "fortunately, on your head." I was knocked unconscious for a couple of hours and when I woke up I was home.

My father said I must have gotten too excited when he said hello to me on television. It gave him a good excuse never to do it again.

The marriage wasn't working out. My father and mother both knew that. So in the fall, after living in it only a few months, they put the Long Island house on the market. My mother and I returned to Florida and my father, having heard good things about California racing, persuaded Mr. Vanderbilt to give it a try.

My father asked my mother not to file for divorce until after the first of the year for tax reasons. She said she wouldn't.

My mother started seeing Larry again. They began to argue. The arguments often got nasty and turned into fights. Finally she broke it off. She began to think that when my father came east in the spring from California she would ask if she might join him. Perhaps it was still not too late. Then my father called and told her she could go ahead and file for the divorce. He would stop by Miami on his way back from California to New York and sign the papers. My mother asked why he was suddenly in such a hurry. He told her he had met a girl.

I also had met a girl. Her name was Sissy. She was brassy, blonde, and could climb a tree or jump off the roof of a new house as well as I could. She was fifteen, six years older than me, a fact she scarcely ever let me forget.

She had already started going out with boys; sometimes they came to pick her up on motor scooters. When she first started dating, she would let me listen on the extension while she talked to them on the telephone. She put a stop to that when I asked her what the University of Miami football player meant when he said "I want you, I want you" in a whispered husky drawl.

About the only one of Sissy's boyfriends I actually got to meet was a tall, sandy haired fellow she called Kansas, I guess because he came from there. He didn't have a motor scooter. It was obvious by the way she talked about him that Sissy had fallen for him.

One Saturday Kansas rented a rowboat to take Sissy to a small, uninhabited island, one of many like it in Biscayne Bay. They were going to have a picnic, they said, and pretend they were explorers on a newly discovered land. At the last minute they invited me to come along.

Kansas did all the rowing. When we got to the island we spread a blanket on the coral rocks—there was no sand—and ate our sandwiches. Afterward Sissy suggested I go see what was on the other side of the island; she and Kansas wanted to "talk." I did as I was told. When I came back twenty minutes later, Kansas and Sissy were glowering at each other. Sissy told me we were leaving.

The splash of Kansas's oars hitting the water was the only sound on the way back to the mainland. Then, about fifty yards before we reached shore, Kansas suddenly dived into the water in all his clothes and swam to the dock. He was waiting for us, wet and grinning, when we got there. When I asked Sissy about it she just shrugged. "He's different, that's all," she said.

Sissy and Kansas went out together for a couple more months. They were always breaking up and getting back together again. One night, a week or so after they had last broken up, Sissy called me on the phone. She was crying. I had to come right over she said. "They've arrested Kansas."

The newspapers the next day were full of the crime. Kansas had gone to the home of a seventy-eight-year-old widow and had robbed her and hatcheted her to death. A neighbor had heard the screams and called the police. The newspapers said that when the police asked Kansas why he had done it, he just grinned.

He never came to trial. He was sent to the asylum for the criminally insane in Chatahoochie. There, we later learned, he was discovered to have a brain tumor nearly the size of a lemon.

In the fall of 1951, I was sent for my fifth-grade year to McDonogh, a military school outside Baltimore, and out of range of any possible divorce cross fire. It was mainly my father's idea. My mother didn't want me to go. My father finally persuaded her it was the best thing for everyone. He told her that if it didn't work out, she could take me back to Miami in a year or so.

My father knew little about schools. He'd last been inside one at the age of fourteen. But McDonogh was well known on the racetrack; any number of horsemen had sent their sons there over the years. Then too, McDonogh was only a few miles down the road from Alfred Vanderbilt's Sagamore Farm, where the stable's broodmares, stallions, and yearlings were kept. My father would be able to combine visits to the farm, inspecting the bloodstock, with visits to me. Best of all, to my father's thinking, the school would insulate me from my mother's maternal indulgences. In short, it would make a man of me.

When he put it that way, I found it difficult to argue. Naturally I wanted to be made a man of. I did not want to leave my mother or my friends in Miami. I was frightened of going to a military school. But I certainly didn't want my father to know that I was afraid. Besides, I had no choice. My father had decided.

My mother drove me from New York to Baltimore for the first day of school. Neither of us said much during the trip. In the parking lot at the school, she told me to be a good boy. She said she knew I would try. I looked at the asphalt and concentrated on not crying. My mother looked away. Then quickly I kissed her good-by and ran into the brick building. I was ten years old and shocked to discover just how terrible it was possible to feel.

The sobs I finally subdued that September morning were never far away those next nine months. Over and over I would tell myself that I was becoming a man, that I must be strong, that my father was counting on me. Then I would recall some sweet gesture of my mother's, some pleasure that had made her smile (or worse, some deceit that I had put over that now, if only I could, I would redeem) and my throat would clog, my eyes would redden, and the tears would flow.

Every day was agony. It began at 6:45 with an electric bell, pain transcribed into sound, that rang not twenty feet from my ear. Its ringing triggered the cacophony of a thousand springs squeaking in a hundred beds as I and ninety-nine other ten-year-olds leaped to the floor. The other boys took reveille as the signal for a competition above and beyond the ordinary demands of a hectic schedule. In their frantic haste they seemed obsessed, as if all they were or all they might become was somehow linked to how fast they could complete their wake-up tasks and get outside for formation. There, of course, they loitered till the time came to "fall in."

Morning "work" followed breakfast. My job was to

sweep out a room full of lockers. It took an hour and I seemed to inhale almost as much dust as I swept up. By the time I finished, the mail would be sorted and I would head, full of hope, to the basement where a post office had been created out of some heavy-gauge wire screening. The *s* and the second *f* on the wooden sign over the mail cage had long since been scraped away, so that it read "Po t Of ice."

We would line up waiting for Mr. Moorhead, the postmaster, to finish sorting the mail. The longer I waited, the more my anticipation built. The greatest prize was a letter from my mother. My father's letters, next best, usually contained a few dollars, always some odd number like three or seven, as if, when he finished writing, he simply reached into his pocket and inserted whatever bills he happened to find.

Within a few weeks, I came to think of Mr. Moorhead as a man of diabolical power, so casually did he manipulate my happiness. Though he knew our names, he insisted that we announce ourselves when we at last arrived at the head of the line.

"Good morning, Mr. Moorhead," I'd say. "Winfrey."

Mr. Moorhead would not look up from the wooden box into which he had just sorted the morning mail. A dirty forefinger would flip to a divider card marked *W*. He'd pull out a bunch of envelopes and glance through them; then, without looking up, he'd pass any letters addressed to me through a narrow opening in the cage. More often he would simply say, "No Winfrey." In such moments I silently cursed him to an everlasting mail line, punctuated only by a vengeful Lord announcing, "No Moorhead."

Elated or disappointed, I would head up six flights of stairs to the dorm to savor any letters I might have gotten. Then I'd shower, change into my uniform, and prepare for inspection. There were three kinds—personal, beds, or lockers. We never knew in advance which it would be that day, though we never gave up trying to outguess our inspectors.

Mr. Mason, who taught science when he was not taking a

dim view of the way I had folded my pajamas, was a beds man. You could count on him to go after beds no less than three times a week. A Mason-approved bed was tight enough to bounce a quarter, wrinkle-free with an eight-inch fold at the head precisely fourteen inches from the end. Square corners on the *sides* not the end, with the extra blanket folded in sixths, the double edge toward the pillow. Watch out for dust on the underside of the frame.

Mr. Walters, essentially a lockers man, had a thing about undershirts: they had to be four inches across with a single fold showing. He also had a special interest in cap visors, which were best polished with a dab of Brylcreem or, in a pinch, with a little oil gleaned from the outside of the nose, just above the nostril.

Mr. Craig favored "personal" inspection—particularly hands. If you had calluses, you were in trouble. Mr. Craig did not admit to the existence of calluses. "That's dirt," he would say. "It'll come off. Try scrubbing." Mr. Craig also insisted on spit-shined shoes and short fingernails. "Hands. Over. Down. About face. Uh-huh. You forgot to shine your heels. Three."

A "three" was fair: no demerits. "Two," unsatisfactory: one demerit. A "one" got you three demerits. On the other side, a "four" was good. "Five," perfect. Nobody had ever seen Mr. Mason give a five for anything. There was a standing joke that on his wedding night Mr. Mason had given his wife a three. (Though I laughed, I did so because I thought his wife hadn't made such a good bed.)

I signed up for riding as my fall sport, thinking that riding at least would be familiar and therefore bearable. I soon learned, however, that riding on the racetrack and riding around a ring in a very proper riding class were quite different matters. I thought posting was an unnecessary nuisance. The fastest gait, a canter, I considered an absurdly tame substitute for the real fun of horses—going flat out.

It is tempting to recall the tall, swarthy boy I met at the riding stable as a friend. But he wasn't, really. Bayswinder seemed as unhappy as I. He was older, a ninth grader. He wore his dark, straight hair long, combed straight across his forehead.

I don't remember how we met, or even if we were ever formally introduced. I remember one afternoon at the stable he needed some saddle soap and asked me for it. He called me "Win-fairy." ("Fairy" was a term we all used without any precise meaning beyond a faint suggestion of sissy.)

But I was more surprised than angry. I didn't know Bayswinder even knew my name. That first time, his voice was edged with hostility. "Hey, Win-*fairy*."

As time passed, we took to nodding at each other. Once he made some vague reference to my father that told me he somehow knew he trained race horses. As time passed, he got friendlier.

"Hi, Winfairy."

"Hi, Bayswinder."

Not much more than that.

We heard the news about a week later, on a Sunday night. Those who had gone home for the weekend were back. The standard Sunday night special—bacon and cheese on stale toast—was the fare; dinner conversations were loud and animated. I was sitting with my back to the door, so it was only by the sudden silence in the dining room that I knew something was up.

It was "Doc," the headmaster, a man of great kindness and energy, feared and revered in the great English headmaster tradition. He knew every boy by his first name. Every boy in turn called him Doc.

Doc's face was ashen, his eyes red. The clatter of silverware in the dining room ceased instantly. The silence was overwhelming.

Finally Doc began to speak. He spoke slowly in a low

voice. He talked about how this school was not just a school but a family. He said that sometimes, immodestly, he got to thinking of all of us as *his* family. But it wasn't his, really. It was all of ours. And what made a family was our willingness to help each other, to look after each other, to take care of each other. Together families took joy in the good, and when the bad times came they helped each other in their sorrow.

Nobody knew why Doc looked the way he did or why he was saying the things he was saying. We knew something terrible must have happened but we didn't know what it could be. Finally Doc got around to telling us. Bayswinder had hanged himself in the stable.

I called my mother in Miami every Monday. I would approach those calls the way a general approaches a battle; but my victories, when they occurred, were over tears. Vowing not to cry, not to tell her how much and how terribly I missed her, I often brought to the pay phone a list of topics to talk about. But more often than not, once I heard her voice, I would forget the list and would begin to tell her, again and again, how much I missed her.

I even took to praying. After taps I'd ask the Lord to help me turn quickly into a man. You see, I'd explain to Him, this homesickness is killing me. I also asked forgiveness for God-only-knows what innocuous transgressions of McDonogh rules I elevated to the status of sin. Finally I prayed that I would not get sick. I was obsessed with the idea that I would get so ill I would not be able to go to Miami for Christmas vacation.

Most afternoons after athletics, I would go to the infirmary. I had aches. I had colds. I had bruises. I had an ingrown toenail that I soaked every day for months in a tub of hot water.

I hated the infirmary. I hated the smell of it and the charts we had to fill out, one line for each visit, fifty lines to a page.

The nurses didn't like me. They didn't like little boys who they thought were inventing pains just so they could come to the infirmary. They thought I was one of those.

But in fact I only went because I thought that if I didn't fill out the chart, and smell those awful infirmary smells, and wait in line until I could tell the head nurse (who insisted on calling me "Win-i-free" as if my name had three syllables) what was troubling me, I would get a tumor in my brain or my bruise would turn gangrenous, and I would die a long way away from my mother.

Shortly after Thanksgiving, I was admitted to the infirmary for what proved to be a painful ordeal. The intestinal grippe had little to do with it. I vomited and I sweated but my real concern was getting out in time for my Monday phone call to my mother. I tried to explain to the nurses that she was expecting me to call, that if I didn't she would worry, she wouldn't know what was the matter.

"Win-i-free," said the head nurse, "we'll take care of it." I knew she wouldn't. I knew that my mother would be home waiting for me to call at my regular time and that when I didn't she would worry. I felt powerless to prevent this terrible thing from happening; it was made all the more terrible—it seemed to me—by its preventability. Monday night I sneaked out of the ward to a phone I had seen in the infirmary office. But before I could dial, I was caught and sent back to bed for a worrisome, sleepless night.

The next morning I was weaker than I had been since I first was admitted. My temperature was up. Late that afternoon, the Officer of the Day came to the infirmary with a message for the nurse: I should call my mother. She was very worried.

In the back of the McDonogh yearbook of 1952 are two blank pages thoughtfully provided by the publisher for notes, witticisms, or comments. I headed one of those pages, "My Class." At the top of the other I wrote "Friends." There are twenty-three signatures under the first heading. There are none under the second.

It was odd, the next year, the way things changed for me—a kind of how to succeed in the lower school without really trying.

The lower school was run by the sixth graders, particularly the commissioned officers: one major, three captains, and ten lieutenants. Almost every sixth grader—unless a new boy, a perpetual screw-up, or some malcontent who refused to play the game—carried some rank. The lowest was private; then corporal.

I was a corporal, or would be once I completed Officers Candidate School. All potential officers and non-coms reported for school a week early for the honor of marching around a hot, tarry drill field with dummy Springfield rifles on our shoulders and attending classes in "M.S. and T"— Military Science and Tactics. I excelled by keeping my shoes and brass polished and turning sharply left when anybody near me hollered "Column left" or right when they yelled "By the right flank . . . March." And I didn't cry; not once. The campus was familiar. I knew most of the other kids. And there was the rank to live up to. Privates may cry. Corporals really mustn't.

At the end of Officers Candidate School, owing to my demonstrated ability to go left and right following the appropriate commands, I was selected by the faculty instructors for promotion to sergeant: three stripes.

The cadet major didn't come back to school that fall; his father, a center fielder for the Philadelphia Phillies had been traded to the Chicago Cubs. The boarding company commander, a captain, moved up to major. One of the boarder lieutenants became a day student. A second got sick and missed Officers Candidate School entirely. Thus, our company suddenly found itself without any commissioned officers at all. Their places would be filled by sergeants. By me!

One week I'd carry out the normal sergeant's function, standing at the rear of the platoon telling Edwards or Peters to quit talkin' or to stand up straight. The next week I'd be a lieutenant, barking commands to my platoon as we marched to meals or during drill. The next week I'd be a captain, the company commander, exalted above my classmates, outranked in the chain of lower-school command only by the cadet major. It was heady stuff.

Those of us in "authority" took our responsibilities seriously. Not only did we devote countless hours to spit-shining our shoes and Brasso-ing our brass, but we also gave considerable energy to fashioning ourselves into authority figures. We took our cues from our older, upper-school counterparts. At least most of us did. I took my cues from Tommy.

Tommy Dale, our cadet, lower school, battalion commander, was a rough-hewn lad from Maryland's eastern shore farm country. His arms and huge, callused hands hung—it seemed to me—nearly to his knees.

Tommy's mother and father had told Tommy a hundred times of the sacrifices they had made to send Tommy to this wonderful school. He had better make the most of it.

Tommy did. Though not the brightest kid in our class, he studied hard; his name appeared regularly on the second honor roll and even, from time to time, on the first.

In the fall he went out for football, the first to arrive at practice, the last to leave. In winter, he wrestled. In spring, he played lacrosse. When he wasn't studying or playing a sport or writing a letter to his parents, he was shining his shoes or his brass. His bed was as tight as a trampoline; his locker repulsed dust. He never lost his "spiffy," the bent wire and spring device we wore under our neckties to keep our collars straight.

I held him in awe. I had never seen such dedication and

purposefulness. Or such authority. "Buoy," he would say in his eastern shore twang, "Buoy, you better watch yourself. If you don't straighten out and straighten out fast, you're gonna have to deal with me. You understan' what I'm sayin' to you, bouy?"

"Yes, sir."

Tommy didn't leave any room for backtalk.

In short order, I took on the more imitable of Tommy's mannerisms, including selected eastern shore pronunciations of words like "bouy" and "schoowal."

My other friend was Samson Romanella. He was short and squat with a turned-up nose.

Samson had no rank, no authority and very little ambition. He did not study hard, his shoes were scruffy. What he did best were things like urinating twelve or fifteen feet over the sinks from one side of the bathroom to the other, and wearing 45 rpm records on his ears at formation just for a laugh. He also cultivated, and I suppose came as close to perfecting as anybody ever has, the ability to upchuck more or less at will, though it was usually right after meals.

The climax of the military year was competition drill. It took place on Memorial Day every year. It was the culmination of all those hours on the drill field and of all the hoarse young voices shouting a field manual of commands, of standing at attention with feet at a forty-five-degree angle, thumbs behind the seams of your pants. It was the climax, too, of the perpetual and at times heated rivalry between the boarding students and the "dayhops," that undisciplined, slovenly horde that piled off yellow school buses each morning.

Having gone leaderless all year, Company E, my company, was virtually written off as serious competition drill contenders. The faculty adviser's reluctance to pick a company commander from among us didn't help our chances at all.

Six weeks before competition drill day I was one of two

sergeants in my company promoted to lieutenant. Clearly one of us would command the company in competition. Each day after that we alternated the captain's position. I geared my whole being to getting that job. Now when reveille rang, I was the first one up, the first dressed, the first to get outside and loiter.

Two weeks before the big day, Major Walsh, the faculty adviser, called me into his office.

"I've been watching you closely," he said to me.

"Yessir," I said.

"You've come a long way this year," he said.

"Yessir," I said. "Thank you, sir."

"Well," he said. "I guess there's no point in making small talk. Congratulations, you will command the company in competition."

My head swam.

Suddenly my ambition knew no bounds. I called the company together in a special formation. "Men," I said in my best Gregory Peck *Twelve O'Clock High* manner, "we are given no chance to win competition drill. But I think we can do it. It will take practice. It will mean drilling every day after school during free time. It'll mean all of us working together." I asked for a show of hands. Every arm was raised.

For the next three weeks I lived, ate, and dreamed competition drill. Each day after school we assembled for two hours' practice. I knew that we had to come up with something dramatic. I went to see an upper-school cadet major whom I'd gotten to know one weekend.

"Well," he said, "there is a maneuver you could try. But it's very difficult."

"I'll try it," I said.

"Okay. It's called 'to the winds': the squad on the right does a 'right flank,' the middle squad goes 'to the rear,' and the squad on the left does a 'left flank.' "

"Great," I said. "Then what happens?"

"Well, when you're spread out the width of the parade

field, you give 'To the rear, march.' If everybody stays covered off and in step, they all turn back to their original directions when they meet in the center."

"Wow," I said. "That sounds terrific."

"It is," said the cadet major. "If it's done right. But if it's not executed perfectly, it's a disaster."

There were only ten days to go. I introduced the new command at drill practice that night. It was a disaster.

It continued a horrible botch, with squads crashing into one another, for a full week. Then, with only a few days to go it began to take shape.

Word leaked to the dayhops that we had a surprise to pull on them. In a desperate effort to match us, they began special practice drills during the lunch hour, trying to perfect another tricky command called "counter march."

The night before the competition drill some of the older upper-school cadets stopped by after taps to wish me luck. "Don't forget to salute the officer who comes to inspect you," said one of them.

Competition drill day was clear and warm. It passed slowly. Finally, at 3:00 P.M., white shirts starched, brass polished to a high gleam, and spit-shined shoes glistening in the sun, we assembled and marched to the fieldhouse monument to pay homage to those McDonogh men who died in World War II. Twenty paces in front of my company I stood at rigid attention, my heart pounding with the drums, as a thousand cameras clicked our picture.

On the parade ground the inspection came first. The Army major was a giant.

"Company E prepared for inspection, sir," I said.

Behind him Major Walsh was gesturing at me with his hand. Of course, I'm going to salute him, I thought, returning Major Walsh's glare, just as soon as the inspector salutes me.

The two of us stared at each other, waiting for the other to lift his arm.

"Well," said the major finally, "let's get on with it."

I followed in tow, realizing my error at last, as the Army man went down the ranks, looking at shoes and rifles, asking the occasional cadet where he hailed from.

When he finished, I saluted. The major smiled and returned my salute.

"Drill your company," he said.

I called them to attention, gave them "Forward, march," and led them easily through a few basic commands. "By the right flank, harch!" "By the left flank, harch!" "To the rear, harch!" My voice settled down. My commands were coming out clear and in control. "You had a good home but you left," I sang and they echoed back, "You're right."

I marched my company to the center of the drill field. I looked out of the corner of my eye to make sure the Army major was watching. Then I took a deep breath. "To the winds, harch!" I bellowed. My company began heading in three directions. It was the most beautiful sight I had ever seen.

"To the rear, harch!" Now came the test. Would they meet together and turn precisely or, as had happened so many times before, would squads collide? They were beyond my control. It was all up to them.

Swish. Ninety cadets pivoted together. In one consummate moment I loved them all, loved the school, loved drilling and commanding, and loved the uniform I wore.

Twenty minutes later our company assembled before a crowd of two thousand parents and alumni while our expectations were confirmed.

"Attention to orders," read the adjutant. "A cup, presented by the American Legion Post to that company in the lower school winning competition drill. Company E, commanded by . . . Lieutenant Winfrey."

"Com-pany," I called. "Tench-hut. Forward at half-step, harch. Company . . . halt. Present . . . arms."

While my company presented arms, I watched with growing trepidation as Major Walsh led a young lady in a chiffon dress across the field. In her hand she carried a silver cup; it looked nearly as big as I was. In growing horror, I saw that she was a good six inches taller than me. How would I ever kiss her?

The hardest part of the afternoon seemed still before me. Do I take the cup first? Or shake Major Walsh's hand first? Or try to kiss the girl first?

"Take the cup in your left hand," Major Walsh said out of the side of his mouth.

"Now shake my hand with your other hand."

"Now I'd like to present Miss Nancy McAlister."

I was on my own. I removed my cap with my right hand and put my arm around her. Then I stood on tiptoe. Then I puckered my lips and, for the first time in my life, kissed a real, live, breathing girl. From the stands I heard an approving murmur, which blended neatly with the snickers to my rear.

Native Dancer was the best horse my father ever trained. When, as a two-year-old in 1952, the Dancer began winning everything in sight, hundreds of thousands of people who had never even been to a racetrack began rooting for him on television.

He was undefeated that year, winning more than a quarter of a million dollars in nine races—eight of them stakes. He was the unanimous choice in all the polls as champion two-year-old and drew Horse of the Year recognition from the wire services.

The "gray ghost from Sagamore" was easy to spot in a race. His finishes were invariably dramatic. He loved to come from far off the pace, often covering enormous distances in the last few hundred yards, bringing onlookers to their feet in living rooms as well as in the grandstand. My father used to instruct Eric Guerin, the Dancer's regular rider, to lay back until the stretch run. The great horse had a tendency to slow down once he took the lead, as if once the challenge were past there wasn't much point in persisting; the idea was to get up his momentum near enough to the finish line so that even if he "stopped" it wouldn't matter—he'd still win.

Native Dancer began racing in the spring of my first year at McDonogh, breaking his maiden with a four-and-a-half-length victory at Jamaica in New York City. Four days later he became a stakes winner, taking the Youthful Stakes by six lengths. But it was not until I left McDonogh for summer vacation that I became aware that my father had a champion in the barn.

At Saratoga that August, where workmen screened off Native Dancer's stall to keep the flies from bothering him—an unprecedented bit of largesse—he won the Flash Stakes, the Saratoga Special, the Grand Union Hotel Stakes, and the Hopeful, all within the space of a month. By the time we returned to Belmont in early September, he had become a celebrity of the first order. As he prepared for the Futurity, I returned to McDonogh, filled with purposeful resolve, and added to my prayers the request that Native Dancer win the Triple Crown. I was very careful about the wording. I never actually asked the Lord to *help* the Dancer—I had enough confidence in the horse—but I implored Him to keep him sound and not to let him get blocked in the stretch.

In the Futurity that fall Native Dancer did get blocked. Eric Guerin said afterward that at the head of the stretch he thought for sure he was beaten. Then he and the Dancer slipped through a small opening to catch the leader, a stepbrother named Tahitian King, and win by two and a half lengths to tie the world record for six and a half furlongs. It was his eighth straight victory with no defeats.

The Dancer won three more stakes that winter. As spring approached, he was far and away the favorite for the 1953 Kentucky Derby.

I knew the Dancer could win. But I worried about my father's Derby luck. His horses either broke down right before the race or, if they started, suffered some quirky misfortune.

The year before he had had to scratch his Derby prospect, a bay colt named Cousin, just a couple of days before the race. Cousin simply and unequivocally refused to train. He wouldn't even gallop around the track in the morning. I well remember the sight of my father, a bull whip hanging from his hand, trying to intimidate Cousin into simply *walking* to the training track for his morning workout. Before that there had been Loser Weeper, the best of his year, who had pulled up lame just a month before the Derby, and Bed O'Roses, who my father had thought might be the first filly since Gallorette to win the Derby. She bowed a tendon two weeks before the race.

The Dancer had a tremendous public following. Bettors had made him one of the biggest favorites ever, with the extremely short odds of three to ten. Ernest Hemingway bet ten thousand dollars on him.

My father had arranged for a friend of his to pick me up at McDonogh that Saturday morning and take me to his home to watch the race on television. My father would call me there after the race and then my father's friend would take me out for a big dinner to celebrate.

I sat three feet from the set as the horses were led into the starting gate. Eddie Blind, the official starter, squeezed the buzzer. "They're off!" said Clem McCarthy, the race announcer.

Native Dancer broke well, in the middle of the bunch. Eric Guerin didn't hit him at all, just threw the reins at him a bit to give him his head. He had settled into his smooth, giant stride, going into the first turn laying an easy fourth, when suddenly a horse called Money Broker swerved sharply, knocking Native Dancer nearly to his knees. When he recovered, he had lost several lengths.

Along the backstretch the Dancer trailed the leaders. Forced wide in the turn, he nonetheless began passing horses. Guerin saw an opening near the rail and eased over to it. Then, as the Dancer inched toward the leader, the hole closed. Guerin swung his mount again outside and called upon him for another drive. Now in the stretch, the great gray colt began passing horses again. As the stands filled with a powerful roar the Dancer, streaking on the outside, seemed to be flying. As they went under the finish line, he swept by Dark Star, the front runner. But not in time. The official photograph showed that Dark Star had won by a neck.

Lester Murray, the Dancer's groom, swears that the horse stopped, turned, and looked wistfully toward the winner's circle as he was being led back to the barn after his first, and only, defeat.

Later my father would say that in the last hundred yards the Dancer had run the fastest he had ever run in his life, faster probably than any racehorse had ever run any time. My father masked his disappointment. "That's horse racing," he would say if anybody ever asked him about the Dancer losing the Derby. And he refused to join in the criticism of Eric Guerin's ride.

I had learned no such stoicism. As I came to the crushing realization that Native Dancer had lost, had irrevocably been beaten and would not win the Triple Crown, my vow never to cry again was forgotten in a rush of tears. Sobbing into my hands, I waited for my father to call me. I expected, somehow, to be comforted. When no call came, I asked my father's friend to please drive me back to McDonogh, and thanks just the same for the invitation to dinner.

In the two years that I was away at McDonogh, Larry had convinced my mother to marry him and begin a new life. She wanted me to be a part of it. My father, who had also remarried, could scarcely object. After all, my mother had kept her part of the bargain by letting me go away to school in the first place. And my father was a man of his word.

He did persuade her, however, to let me spend the intervening summer in New York with him. His new wife, Elaine, and her two boys would not be coming east till

August. In the meantime we would share a room at Belmont Park on Long Island in the new brick quarters built for the help right next to the stable.

It wasn't very good, living almost on top of each other in one small room. I couldn't get used to my father's snoring. He couldn't get used to me. He found me whiny and petulant. I found him austere and overbearing.

"We don't seem to have much fun together any more," I said to him one morning after some meaningless argument.

"Fun?" he said. "I'm your father. Fathers aren't *for* fun."

But another morning—we had just finished saddle-soaping our shoes at the end of the working day (another ritual upon which my father insisted)—my father surprised me by reaching into his pocket and throwing the car keys my way.

"Back her out and bring her around," he instructed me.

I could hardly believe my ears. My father actually trusting me with his new station wagon. Perhaps I had judged him too harshly; I saw possibilities of a whole new relationship.

My heart was beating with pride as I started the car. I looked into the rear-view mirror and touched my foot to the accelerator. When I heard the crrrrrunch I gasped. The fender had folded like a piece of cardboard. I sat, stunned, not knowing what to do, waiting for the inevitable. But my father didn't come running around the barn, madder than hell. He didn't jerk open the car door, yanking me out by the arm. Nothing. Nothing happened.

I put the car in drive and inched it forward, releasing the fender from the post. Then, very cautiously, I backed the car out, realizing as I did so that if my father was still standing where I had left him, talking to the foreman under the shed, the smashed fender would be on his far side. He might not see it. It was a risk, but considering the alternatives I felt it was worth taking.

With sweating hands I put the car in drive once more and stepped lightly on the accelerator. Though my plan was still forming, I knew that everything depended on my acting as normally as possible. I braked in front of the barn. My father stood where I had left him.

"About time," he said. "What kept you?"

"Oh, nothing," I said. Since I was often vague, my father accepted the answer.

I quickly opened the door for him and slid over to the other side of the front seat. I didn't want to give him a chance to offer to let me drive some more.

My father, still talking to the foreman, got in the car. We drove away. I did my best to keep up my side of the conversation.

We pulled in to a diner for breakfast and parked. I bit my tongue as we walked in front of the car to go inside.

When we had finished and had come outside again, I was the one to spot the damage.

"Oh, no," I cried out. "Look!"

My father kept his anger controlled. "I'll be a sonofabitch," he said. "Damn."

Then he started talking about responsibility and ethics: how a life without them, without a clear and ongoing sense of right and wrong, was not worth living.

"Whoever did this," he said, "may think he's gotten away with something. Sure, he doesn't have to pay the hundred bucks it'll cost to have it fixed. But let me tell you something, son. He's lost a lot more than a hundred dollars. He's lost a part of himself. Every man has to look at himself every morning when he shaves. And what he sees in the mirror, that's what's important."

I wondered if my father somehow knew what I had done and had chosen this subtly effective way to punish and teach me. But knowing what his reaction would have been had he really known, I discounted that theory. Perhaps it was God, I thought, meting out instant retribution through my father.

For a long time I feared that the incident had defined the limits of my courage.

We spent most of that August in Saratoga in a house on Saratoga Lake. My father bought a small boat with an outboard motor and let me have the run of the lake. It was almost ideal, going to the track with him in the morning, waterskiing and swimming in the afternoon.

But it was the first time I had lived with my father's new family. Elaine arrived with her two sons, each about half my age. My father and Elaine were very much in love. Their open affection and the childish delight they took in each other confused me. My father, who was in the process of adopting the two boys, insisted they call him Dad. But I refused to call Elaine Mother, despite his urgings to do so. I didn't like having to eat with the "children." I didn't like "playing" with them. Two older boys lived next door. I much preferred their company. While my father went to the races in the afternoons, I spent a lot of time driving the boat around the lake by myself.

The two brothers built a wooden ski jump ramp, and my father would not be content until he had successfully gone over it. He made it on his fifth try. I was terrified of the jump but at his urging finally agreed to give it a try. As the boat sped toward it, the ramp loomed like a cement wall in my vision. My only consolation was that soon it would be over. My skis hit the jump, there was a loud sound of scraping, and suddenly I was in the air, my skis trailing behind me. I hit the water with a smack, letting go of the rope.

On the next try my ski tips hit the water first, propelling me hard into the water. My face hit flat and I came up spitting blood. I knew that I couldn't make the jump—I simply was not sufficiently in control of my body. But I made twelve attempts that afternoon. Finally my father was convinced that it was beyond my physical capabilities. He said well, at least I wasn't a quitter. In fact, I was simply more afraid of him than of the jump.

My father and I left Saratoga a week early to go to Chicago to run Native Dancer in the American Derby. My father flew out; I took the train, riding with the great horse in a special horsecar. Since losing the Kentucky Derby, the Dancer had won the Preakness and Belmont, the other two legs of the Triple Crown, as well as three other big races including the Travers. But my father wanted to win this Chicago race very badly, I think because it was a Derby.

My father was one of about fifty people, most of them newsmen, who met the train when it pulled into a siding at Washington Park racetrack in Chicago. He told me he was worried because Eric Guerin had been suspended for ten days and would not be able to ride the Dancer in the American Derby. My father had gotten Eddie Arcaro, probably the best jockey in the world, to agree to ride him, but still he was worried. No one but Guerin had ever ridden Native Dancer.

I had a wonderful time in Chicago, tagging along with a photographer and a reporter from *Life* magazine as they worked on a story about my father's horse. My only worry was the same as my father's, that Eddie Arcaro, good as he was, had never ridden the Dancer before.

Arcaro was worried too. He had injured his knee going into a starting gate a couple of weeks before and now an infection had set in. It was swollen and sore. The day before the race, Arcaro had his knee lanced and drained. He showed up the next morning walking stiff-legged and in obvious pain.

Just before the race Arcaro went to the racetrack doctor to get a shot of Novocaine. Arcaro told my father as he was getting on the horse that the Novocaine didn't seem to be having much effect but that he thought he'd be okay anyway.

The Dancer broke poorly and stayed pretty well back all along the backstretch and into the far turn heading for home. My father, who never was very demonstrative in rooting for his horses, began to bark out orders that only I could hear: "Move on him, dammit; let's go."

Suddenly Arcaro seemed to respond and a gray streak broke through the pack. He won going away.

"He's everything they've said about him," Arcaro said afterward. "Sheer power is the only way to describe him." The Dancer had set a track record.

The next morning my father's greatest fear came true. The Dancer was sore; he had bruised his left forefoot. When my father found out that the management of Washington Park had ordered that the track be rolled to make it hard and fast—they wanted a world record—my father was furious. He said he would never run a horse at that racetrack again.

I returned to Miami to reenter Country Day for the seventh grade in the fall of 1953. My mother dyed my military dress shirts pink and enrolled me in the Miami Shores Country Club cotillion.

It was an awkward time: I still wore braces on my teeth; my face had begun its decade-long battle with acne; and my voice seemed to be thinking about changing. Yet I managed at the very first of those dreadful dancing classes to tumble hopelessly in love.

Her name was Regina. At thirteen she was poised, beautiful, and out of the question.

She found me amusing. She laughed at the funny things I stayed up nights thinking to say to her on the telephone, spontaneously, the next day. Her laughter fueled my ardor and blinded me to the impossibility of my dream: to "go steady." That I adored her she was undoubtedly aware. But with the insight into men that some women seem born with, she struck a balance between intimacy and distance by making me her confidant.

It was partly to impress my friends that I invited her to a party at my cousin Judy's house on Biscayne Bay. Judy was in love also. Lincoln, a year ahead of me in school, was the all-around boy for whom everything comes too easily. Rich, tall, with an electric smile, he maintained the only elegant ducktail haircut in Miami. He made top marks and captained the eighth-grade football, basketball, and baseball teams.

I think both Judy and I must have realized our chances with our love objects had vanished from the moment we introduced them. From their first sight of each other Lincoln and Regina knew they had at last found what they were looking for. From that evening on they were the unquestioned beautiful couple of our small, unreal Miami world.

Regina lived with her father, a strict man who allowed her no dates on school nights and insisted she be home by 11:00 P.M. on weekends. Regina spent Sundays with her mother, a lovely woman whose low self-esteem had been determined by an unfortunate series of collisions with life in which she had been the loser. She had even lost custody of her only child. With her shrunken ego, she could not find it in herself to refuse her daughter's request to share her Sundays with Lincoln.

I was usually invited along, perhaps as company for her mother. We comprised a bizarre foursome: one love-struck couple and a chaperone from each generation. We went to the movies, where Regina's mother and I feigned absorption in the carryings-on of Rock Hudson and Doris Day while our attention actually focused on the more explicit lovemaking taking place in the seats between us.

Why did I torture myself by tagging along those Sundays? Perhaps just to be near this golden couple. I suppose I was also the victim of a line of 1950s Hollywood logic in which the heroine is betrayed by her lover and turns at last to her loyal friend, a patient stalwart whose unselfish love finds its reward just before the closing credits. Though I would never admit wanting Regina to be betrayed by Lincoln, I thought I ought to be handy just in case.

By this time I had turned into a kind of walking erogenous zone. Acting on whims and motives discernible only to itself, my penis swelled to erection a dozen times a day—at movies, while walking down the street, on buses.

I had devised a masturbation "kit": nothing formal—a

tube of Brylcreem ("a little dab'll do ya") and some nudist colony magazines filched from a local newsstand. To this basic collection was eventually added a strange little foldout pamphlet, a yard long but no more than three inches high, that depicted fauns, leprechauns, and other manner of strange beasts cavorting in various Dionysian exercises. To my thirteen-year-old eyes, it looked more like animals, devils, and masked men with huge penises. I had found it in my new stepfather's dresser drawer, under his socks.

It wasn't long before my mother came around to ask if I had, by any chance, taken something of Larry's, a little foldout collection of animals. No, I hadn't. Was I sure? Sure I was sure. She believed me. I had never lied to her. She believed that too.

It was about six weeks later that she found the "kit"— Brylcreem, leprechauns, and all. She was waiting for me when I got home from school. She marched me upstairs to confront me with the evidence. Then she came at me with an open hand that frightened me less than her loss of control; she was shrieking and crying and hitting me all at the same time. My mother, always so beautiful, had turned ugly, her mouth and face contorted into expressions I had never seen. Through the tirade I managed to deciper that it was not the nudes or the Brylcreem or even taking the pamphlet that bothered her so much. It was the lying.

"How could you, how could you?" she said over and over again, as I could only burble how sorry I was, please forgive me. I cried most of that night and then stopped. I didn't masturbate for a month.

I had known Simon for years. We had been rivals more than friends, probably because we were so much alike. But when I returned to Florida as a winning company commander, I no longer felt threatened by him. Simon and I were like those little black and white scottie magnets kids used to have; if the scotties were placed tail to tail, they repelled each other. Turned around, they attracted. Somehow, during the two years I had been away, Simon and I got turned around. We fed each other's rebelliousness: we prowled neighborhoods and broke into houses; we threw baby coconuts and sometimes rocks at passing automobiles; we stole a car, went for a joy ride and got it back before the owner ever missed it. When we saw Marlon Brando in *The Wild One,* we left the movie keyed up and anxious to do something "tough." Simon remembered that he had packs of firecrackers and cherry bombs at his house. We went to get them and took them all into the dark corridor of a big public school. We made a long fuse. The first explosion nearly knocked us off our feet. Those firecrackers just kept going and going like gangsters with Tommy guns. When the police cars started showing up, we ran like hell. For a while there we never got caught at anything we did.

Miami Country Day ended after the eighth grade.

Both my mother and father showed up for my graduation. They managed to be civil through it all. Afterwards, my father took me to the barbershop for a crewcut. His one concession was to let me have a flat-top. It looked ridiculous. Then he and I together drove across the state, Florida, to the west coast where he had arranged for me to work at an experimental marine biology laboratory owned and funded by the owner of the horses he then trained.

Living in a rundown motel in what was then a desolate area filled with pine scrub and gray sand, I spent most of my after-hours time writing long, tortured letters to Regina back in Miami.

I skindived, preserved fish in formalin, dissected a bat, boiled a tarpon's head until all the bones came loose (and tried unsuccessfully to put it all back together again), and fell in love with my boss, Eugenie Clark, who was much too pretty to be an ichthyologist.

In the fall I returned to McDonogh for my four high school

years. Tommy and Samson filled me in on all the gossip I had missed in the two years I had been away. The three of us were among about a dozen students chosen to be lower school "daddies" and assigned to live with and look after the younger cadets. I went to the Big Wing, my old home, to look after fifth and sixth graders. I had thus returned to McDonogh a counselor to my former self.

McDonogh was now comfortable. I understood its rules and lived happily within them. McDonogh made me feel safe and secure. It was home and I was grateful for it. Perhaps that is why it is the summers between those years that I remember best.

I spent the summer of 1956 working at a thoroughbred horse farm in Ocala, Florida. My father had arranged the job for me.

"A little hard work'll be good for you," he said. He was right about the hard work part: up at five to muck out a dozen stalls and brush and clean as many horses, I rarely finished my stable duties much before noon. After an hour's lunch break, I joined the farmhands in the hay fields, hefting hundred-pound bales onto a flatbed truck that followed along behind the baler. The sun burned through my shirt and the hay mingled with my sweat.

But I was healthy and fairly strong and soon got used to it. And I made friends, particularly with the farm manager's son, Lucas. Lucas was nineteen, four years older than me, blond, bright, and a breaker of hearts at the University of Florida, where he was studying to be a veterinarian. He took it as a solemn obligation to lead me astray.

He invited me to go with him to a place he knew " 'bout fifty miles down the road. Music, booze, girls." He made his eyebrows go up and down and smiled.

I could hardly wait till Saturday night. We had no sooner headed out, Lucas at the wheel, than he turned to me.

"You chugalug?" he said.

"What?" I said.

"You chugalug?" he repeated.

"Oh, yeah," I said. "Sure. Sure I do."

Lucas pulled out a quart of vodka in a brown paper bag from the back seat. He turned the radio up, opened the Ford up to about seventy-five, and took two or three gulps from the bottle. He belched, wiped his lips with the back of his hand, and passed the bottle on to me. I looked at it, wiped the bottle's mouth with the palm of my hand as I had seen it done in the movies, closed my eyes, and swallowed. I gasped. But when Lucas looked at me, grinning, I took another swallow. And another. "Euumhh," I said, coughing. "Mighty good!" I passed the bottle back to Lucas.

In this fashion we consumed the quart of vodka and the fifty miles. We went from gleeful anticipation ("Gonna get us some poontang tonight, you bet!") to robust camaraderie ("Y'know, Lucas, you're a good ole shit, y'know that?"), to . . .

Then it hit me. My eyes swam. The car whirled around me. I reached out to hold onto the dash.

"Lucas," I said, "I don't feel so good."

Lucas wasn't feeling much by that time either, but he still had his senses about him.

"Here we are," he said. "Get some fresh air. You'll feel better."

I did feel a little better, even managed to stagger inside the roadhouse to express a dim view of the way these folks "bopped." At some point in the evening I even insisted on demonstrating the right way to do it.

My memory picks up again on the way home. I am in the front seat but now there is a girl between Lucas, who is driving, and me; in the back seat, another couple. All four of them are singing very near the top of their lungs and swilling vodka from a new bottle. I am neither singing nor swilling. I am holding on to the seat and to the armrest and am concentrating very hard on not throwing up.

By the time we reached the outskirts of Ocala, the mood in the car had changed. Singing and swillings had given way to nuzzlings and rubbings. I was the only one alone. I sulked. Without effect.

"Well," I said suddenly, "I can see when I'm not wanted." I opened the door and stepped out of the car. It happened too fast for Lucas to put on the brakes, but I was too drunk or too lucky to be hurt. I tumbled a couple of times before coming to a stop on the shoulder of the road.

Lucas stopped the car. He and his friend picked me up and carried me, protesting, back to the car. They delivered me to the little motel where I lived, and when I insisted I would be all right they drove off into the night.

It all came clear to me as they drove off: I was the pimply-faced outsider, doomed to repel women, unable even to chugalug. My course was clear: I must lie down on the highway and await my fate.

It was late. There weren't many cars on the road. Lucas found me. He had taken his girl home, then thought he'd just better check on me.

Once Lucas left again, I staggered the mile or two to the farm where we worked, stole a jeep, and headed for the Chicken Ranch, the local Coke-and-hamburger drive-in hangout where my alcohol-soaked brain had some vague idea about picking up a girl and redeeming my manhood.

But halfway to the Chicken Ranch I had to pull over. The time, at last, had come to heave my guts. I thought the marrow in my bones would come up. I stood weakly, reeking of vomit, suddenly mortified in sobriety. Shamefaced, and for the first time terrified at what I might have done to myself, I returned the jeep and tiptoed home to await a monumental hangover.

Native Dancer had returned to racing in the spring. After easily winning the Commando Purse, he carried 130 pounds in the Metropolitan Handicap at Belmont Park in New York.

It was in that race that John Hay Whitney said he hoped the Dancer would beat his own horse, Straight Face. At the head of the stretch, with less than a quarter of a mile to the finish, Straight Face led by seven lengths. Suddenly a gray streak appeared on the outside. When it was over, Native Dancer had won by half a length.

My father wanted to take him to Europe in the fall, where racing is vastly different, in order to prove that he was the finest thoroughbred in the world. He particularly had his eye on the Prix de l'Arc de Triomphe. I got a passport. We might even stay a while, my father said.

I went to Saratoga in August. In the Oneonta Handicap there, the Dancer carried a crushing 137 pounds. I was there to see him win by nine lengths. It would be his last race.

The next morning my father came back from the barn looking very tired. Native Dancer had bruised his forefoot again. Alfred Vanderbilt read a statement to the press: "After working out this morning, Native Dancer showed a recurrence of his former injury. There appears to be no choice but to retire him from racing. He will not race again and will enter stud at the Sagamore Farm in Maryland next spring." He had won twenty-one out of twenty-two races.

I put my passport away and got ready to go back to school in Miami.

It was the next summer that I lost my virginity. I was working in Miami driving a brand-new 1957 "courtesy car" for a Chrysler-Plymouth dealer who was a friend of the family. That was where I met Mose, a University of Miami freshman who was working that summer as a mechanic at the same shop. Sometimes after work we'd head off together for a couple of beers to a place that didn't check ID's too carefully.

One Friday night we found ourselves in a seedy part of downtown Miami in a dime-a-dance hall. Mose had it on good information that the place was stocked with willing women. What it turned out to be stocked with was middle-aged couples practicing the rhumba. We sipped our beers and watched for a while. Then Mose, in a burst of bravado, vowed "to get laid before this night is out." I joined in the vow. I had two dollars and thirty-two cents in my pocket. Mose had four dollars even. I immediately put in a call to a friend named Simon, who was always good for ready cash.

At first we wouldn't tell him what we wanted it for, no doubt to arouse his curiosity.

"Well, if you must know," I finally said to him, "Mose and I are going to get laid tonight."

Simon said he could dig up some money. But of course he would have to come along.

Because Mose boasted of vast sexual experience, the duties of negotiating with doormen and elevator operators fell to him. He had no success at either the Wainstall or the Broadway, both rundown downtown hotels of the kind familiar to every middle-sized American city. Simon and I were just beginning to despair when we saw Mose heading toward us from the Riva Arms, wearing the kind of grin known as "shit-eating." My hands immediately went clammy.

"We're in business," said Mose. He told us we were supposed to wait in the car; Dolores, for that would be her name, would be along shortly. Thirty bucks for the three of us, he said, including the hotel.

"A pretty good deal, huh?" Mose smiled.

We were debating which of us should go first when Dolores appeared.

My hands got clammier. Our Dolores, for whom we had saved ourselves these many years, was a great sea beast of a woman, a veritable leviathan who would top the scales well over two hundred pounds.

"Hi ya, fellas," she said. "Out on the town, are ya?"

"Uh, yes, ma'am," I chirped. Simon and Mose gave me a look that asked if I'd checked my brains with the doorman.

Then it was quiet.

"You got the room?" Dolores asked.

"Three-oh-five," said Mose.

"Well, if it's all the same to you, I think I'll go on up. You got the money?"

Mose handed over the remaining twenty dollars. He'd already given the bellhop ten for the room and his services.

After a minute or two we followed her discreetly into the lobby to continue in whispered tones our discussion over who was to go first. I wanted to beat Simon in losing my virginity. But I didn't feel much like facing Dolores. We were about to draw straws when the bellhop came over.

"Dolores says the one in the red shirt goes first."

That meant Simon.

Forty minutes later he returned, a silly smile on his face. Mose had decided I would go next. I walked slowly to the elevator, feeling like a condemned man. I walked to room 305 and knocked on the door.

"It's open, sweetie," said a voice from inside.

She was lying on the bed in her nightgown, talking on the telephone. I was more shocked by her girth than her nakedness. The idea of screwing this behemoth seemed about as plausible as harpooning a whale from a rowboat.

"Take your clothes off, honey," she said when she had finished talking to her sister. Meekly, I obeyed, stripping to my underpants.

"Your friend told me he was a cherry," she said. "You too?"

"Uh, no. I've had a little experience," I lied.

"Well, fine. That's just fine. In that case let's get started. Come over here and lie down by me."

Again I obeyed. She made me take off my underpants. In time I was hard. In another moment, I was inside her. The first thing that struck me was how warm it was in there. That was the big surprise.

So this is it, I kept saying to myself. My God, I'm doing it. I'm actually doing it!

"Well?" Dolores said, interrupting my self-congratulations.

"What is it?"

"Well, what are you waiting for?"

"Uh, nothing. I mean . . ."

She must have understood. "You've got to move," she said. "Here, like this."

In a little while I was done. She kissed my forehead.

"You did fine," she said. I told her she did too and I meant it.

We went with the whores a few times after that in the cheap hotels in downtown Miami. We learned where to go to find girls who worked across the bay in Miami Beach at twice the price—good-looking some of them were—who came over to Miami on slow nights. I even fell for one of them, a shy young girl from Atlanta who said she was only doing it until she had enough cash to go back to college. They all had a story, of course, but I believed her.

Later that same summer I went to jail.

It happened one Friday night. As usual, neither Mose nor I had a date. We decided to go to a drive-in movie in Mose's car. It was only on the way that he suggested getting some booze. He had been to a party where they'd served this terrific new drink.

"Screwdrivers," he said. "Vodka and orange juice, but you don't taste the vodka."

"No vodka for me," I said, remembering my first and only encounter with the Soviet Union's national drink.

"Suit yourself," he said. "But believe me, you can't even taste the vodka."

He was right. I couldn't. Nor could I tell how drunk I was getting. I just thought the movie was getting funnier. Driving back, I don't think I noticed much of anything until I tried to get out of the car once the cop had pulled us over. When I fell on the ground in front of his feet, I knew we were in trouble.

The cop didn't ask many questions. He left the car by the side of the road and told us to get into the back of the squad car. He took us to Youth Hall, jail for juveniles. We were fingerprinted and booked. They took our belongings for safekeeping. Then they asked for our belts and shoelaces.

"What for?" I asked.

"Shut up," I was told.

Later, in the showers, Mose explained that they took our belts and shoelaces so we wouldn't hang ourselves. That and the hot water sobered me up pretty good.

"Close your eyes," said an attendant as he poured a strong disinfectant on our heads. Mose didn't hear him.

"What?" he said, and the stuff poured into his eyes.

I was taken to a small cubicle with bunk beds and bars on the window. The door was iron, except for a small opening also covered by bars.

I thought of my mother and what she would say when the cops called her. They were probably calling her right now. And I thought about Sunday, and my plane reservation to California to visit my father. If I wasn't out by then, if my father finds out about this, I thought, I've had it.

It seemed I had just gone to sleep when I was awakened by the sound of hollering down the hall. It was morning. I leaped to the little window in the door and saw a man walking toward me down the hall and yelling "Inspection, inspection."

I dressed in a frenzy, thinking that my McDonogh training was coming in handy. I made my bunk in the military manner in less than a minute. Then I heard a key in the door.

A second man, big and ugly, charged through the door. I stood at attention.

"What's this?" he said, looking enraged.

"Ready for inspection, sir," I said.

"Why you wise-ass bastard," he said. He reached down and swooped up my mattress. He threw it at me, hitting me in the chest with it. I fell against the wall.

"Next time, you little wise-ass," he said, "you better have that goddam mattress *off* the bed."

In a little while they came by and unlocked the doors. The two guards, each wearing a pistol and carrying a pipe, stood at either end of the hallway. I stuck my head out the door to see my fellow prisoners walk out and stand in front of their rooms. I did the same, catching a glimpse of an abject Mose across the hall a few rooms down.

On some unseen signal, we turned and followed one of the men single file down a flight of stairs into a room, bare except for a large, plain table. Once seated, I looked over my fellow captives. We were all male, all under eighteen years old. No one spoke. The youngest, a wiry little fellow, looked about twelve. Across from me a mongoloid sat forking lumpy mashed potatoes into his smiling mouth as if it were a Thanksgiving dinner. At the head of the table the guard who had thrown me across the room gnawed on a greasy pork chop bone. I saw now that he had a ragged scar down his cheek. It all seemed a gruesome joke. What in the hell, I asked myself, am I doing here?

I gagged on the potatoes. They tasted of chalk. As if reading my mind, the guard gave me a look of contempt.

"You take it, you eat it," he said. I forced the food down.

After "breakfast" we were led back upstairs, then sent to our rooms to get the toothbrushes we had been issued when we were booked. We lined up at the lavatory door, where the mongoloid, still grinning, squeezed an inch of toothpaste onto our brushes. I was brushing my teeth when I spotted Mose heading for a urinal. As there was a vacancy beside him, I quickly rinsed out my mouth and walked over to it. I had just started to whisper "How're you doin' " when Scarface was upon me, yanking me by the shirt collar and dragging me back to my room, swearing at me. He threw me onto the floor in the room.

"If I catch you layin' on that bed," he said, "I'll break your legs."

He slammed the door behind me. There was no furniture so I sat on the floor and began to cry. Later in the day, I was taken downstairs to meet with my mother. She too had been crying.

She said that a lawyer friend was doing everything possible to get me out. But I'd be there at least until Monday because they didn't release anyone during the weekend. Then she paused and looked me hard in the eyes.

"I'm calling your father," she said, shaking her head to cut off anything I might say. "I can't handle this by myself, Carey. I've tried, but I can't."

I was led back up to my room and sat on the floor. At dinner I elected not to eat at all. This seemed to infuriate Scarface. He stared at me through most of the meal. I looked at my plate.

The next morning, Sunday, we were led after breakfast to a large room I hadn't seen before: the "lounge." We filed into the first three of six rows of folding chairs, filling them. To my surprise, from another door came an almost equal number of girl prisoners. They filled in the rows behind us.

For a few minutes we sat there silently waiting. Then two people filed in, a man of about fifty carrying an accordion and a slender woman of about twenty-five with a trumpet. Both wore the uniform of the Salvation Army. They passed out hymnals and told us to turn to hymn number such-and-such.

The woman with the trumpet began to play off-key. The man with the accordion played and sang. No one joined him. His eyes looked nervously around. Behind me I heard a giggle and a titter. Suddenly it all seemed so ridiculous I wanted to laugh. For the first time in two days I knew I would survive.

The man from the Salvation Army said he knew we could do better than that so let's turn in our hymnals to page so-and-so. This time a few voices were heard above the accordion and trumpet.

Next, the man from the Salvation Army asked us if we had any requests. I raised my hand, having come across a title I thought fitting. It was a hymn about the afterlife—the title was something about how wonderful everything would be when we left this place. When I raised my hand I heard a disapproving murmer behind me. Apparently I had broken some unwritten rule.

But the man from the Salvation Army seemed pleased and he joined me in song. We were the only two singing now and I felt foolish. But I kept at it because I wanted the others to catch on to the irony of the lyric. In a little while another voice joined in, then a third. Finally a chorus swelled as we came to the refrain about how happy we'd be to leave this place.

When we had finished singing, the man asked for another request. A girl behind me asked again for the hymn we had just finished. This time we practically shook the walls with our voices. The man from the Salvation Army didn't know whether to be pleased or put out. When we finished, he just said that would be all and packed up his accordion. But the woman with the trumpet turned around and smiled as she left.

The next morning Mose and I went to a hearing before the judge. Our mothers sat behind us. The judge was kindly. He let us off with some sort of suspended sentence.

The following day I got on a plane to California to face my father. My stepmother met me at the plane. She came running at me and gave me a big hug and a kiss. It was the warmest she had ever been. My father surprised me even more. He did not seem angry: he said I had made a mistake and had been punished for it. He said that everyone was entitled to a mistake. We will see what happens now, he said.

But if I made any more mistakes he would take me out of McDonogh.

I stayed in California a month. It was one of the most pleasant times my father and I ever spent together. My father and I shared a cottage on the beach at Del Mar, about fifty miles south of Los Angeles, for the August meeting at the track there. Elaine stayed in Los Angeles with the children. In the mornings we went together to the track, where I rode Rusty. We spent the afternoons swimming, sunning, and playing volleyball. It was a nice month.

In Miami for Christmas six months later I read in the newspaper that Scarface was dead, stabbed several times by a "deranged youth" who had stolen a knife from the Youth Hall dining room. When I read the item in the paper I thought to myself that the kid who did it, whoever he was, couldn't have been too deranged after all.

I guess the worst thing I ever did was wreck all those golf-mobiles at Vailmont Country Club in Miami Beach. The night it happened Simon and Mose and I were at a party and got to drinking. First thing we knew Mose was telling us he was pretty sure that Vailmont didn't lock its golf carts up at night.

"I bet we could go over there," he said, "take one out, ride it around a while, and nobody'd ever know."

I said sure, why not.

The moon was full that night. The three of us had no trouble making our way to the place where the golfmobiles were stored. There must have been forty of them.

At first we just rode around the course in separate carts. We had a race which Simon won, then another. Then one of us, it may have been me, turned his cart over in a sand trap. The three of us tried to get it righted but finally we gave up. I went back to get another cart.

By the time I came back, Mose had tipped his over too—intentionally. Now he was heading to get another cart.

We decided to race again. Mose got in front of Simon and cut him off when he tried to pass. In the next race Simon got even and rammed Mose at the finish line. After that it turned into a free-for-all. We began ramming each other like bumper car drivers at an amusement park. It had turned into a terrible game: put the other guy out of commission. And the longer it continued, the less we thought about what we were doing, the less concerned we became with right or wrong. Making a great deal of noise without attracting any attention reinforced the sense of unreality.

When the last of some forty golfmobiles lay wrecked on a ravaged golf course, we suddenly shrunk to our normal sizes, then smaller, afraid and humiliated, each desperately eager to be away from the other two.

The newspapers the next afternoon bannered our savage exploit: "Vandals Attack Vailmont." With a mixture of awe, shame, and panic we scanned each succeeding story to read of a massive police investigation and a ten-thousand-dollar reward put up by irate members of the club for any information leading to our capture. Everywhere I went, it seemed, the attack on the golf course was the major topic of conversation. I could not identify with the "vandals," the "criminals," and the "misfits" who had so little regard for property and for the rights of others. I even found myself shaking my head and joining in their condemnation.

My mother discovered a collection of newspaper clippings about the case hidden in my bureau. She was instantly suspicious, but I told her that I had kept them because I was pretty sure that a friend of mine had been involved. I named a wild sort of kid who had often been in trouble. She seemed satisfied.

I sweated it out in Miami for two weeks until at last it came time for me to go north to spend August in Saratoga.

I stayed that summer with my aunt and uncle in Saratoga. The first thing my uncle wanted to know about was the "attack" on Vailmont. He was a member of the club and had read about it in *The New York Times*. He was very upset.

"How could people act that way?" he asked me.

"I don't know," I said. I shook my head.

"I'd sure like to get my hands on whoever did it," he said.

I didn't say anything.

A few words about my uncle: he had been orphaned very early and had grown up at Boys' Town, the famous Father Flanagan home in Kansas. In succession he had been a professional basketball player (he was the shortest man on the original Boston Celtics—a team so good it was disbanded to give the other teams a chance), a bookie, a gambler, an oil speculator, and a racehorse owner, the last three concurrently. My grandfather trained his horses throughout most of the 1950s and was scared to death of him. Whenever my Uncle Eddie called him on the phone, my grandfather practically had apoplexy. His hands already shook from Parkinson's disease and when my uncle called my grandfather's arms and hands flopped around like a man having a seizure.

My uncle was a dark-haired, square-jawed man who resembled James Cagney. When I was growing up in Miami, we would occasionally have dinner at my aunt and uncle's house in Miami Beach. I would sit there, most uncomfortable, as my uncle dominated the table conversation. He could be crude as well as cruel, and he often berated my aunt in front of us all. I thought him a classic sonofabitch.

The last time I saw my uncle was in a bar in New York City. My uncle had put up the money for the bar, helping a young narcotics detective he knew get started in a new business off the force.

My aunt and uncle had been divorced since the last time I had seen him, and I almost didn't recognize my uncle that night, sitting there thin, his skin gray, his eyes myopic behind thick lenses. He was nearly blind from cataracts and certainly didn't recognize me. But when we were reintroduced he insisted on buying me a drink.

We had two or three drinks together. My uncle began to confide in me. He said that he couldn't understand what had happened to him. He had worked hard. He had tried hard. He had made a lot of money. Now here he was at the end of his life: alone, lonely, and unhappy. The only thing anyone wanted from him was his money. He stared at the top of the bar.

"I just can't understand it," he said slowly.

I didn't know what to say. I told him I didn't understand it either. What I did know, I said, was that I had always been afraid of him. The last thing I ever thought he could be, I told him, was sad or lonely or unhappy. I said that I had always thought of him as very strong, tough.

"You've gotta be tough," he said, looking gray and afraid. "In this world you've gotta be tough."

Suddenly I felt very sympathetic toward this old man. Perhaps it wasn't too late, even now, for us to form some kind of friendship. We could have dinner together sometime. Go to the theater.

He said that would be wonderful.

"You know," he said, "I've got this apartment. I pay eight hundred dollars a month for it. New building. Top floor. View of the park. And nobody except the maid has ever been inside it. Nobody's even *seen* it."

"I'll see it," I said. "I'll come by one night and pick you up and we'll go out to dinner and see a show."

"Yes," he said. "That would be nice. Please do that."

I said I would call him next week.

But the next week I was very busy. And the week after that, though I found time to go out with a girlfriend, I postponed calling my uncle. I kept meaning to call him right up until the time he died a couple of months later.

IV

Except for the war years and a couple of others when my father first settled in California, I spent almost every August in Saratoga until I was seventeen. About a dozen, I suppose. A year of Augusts.

The people who live year-round in Saratoga say that the town in August is not Saratoga at all. The rest of the year, they say, it is a quiet college town, with a main street like Main Street and Kiwanis Clubs and PTAs.

The Saratoga I know is more like a carnival town than a college town. Sitting at the corner of Fifth and Lake, Mike Kiley, Joe Toussant, and I could record all forty-eight states from passing license plates in a week of morning monitoring. Saratoga is cool in the mornings and hot in the afternoons, and the people who live near the racetrack park cars on their front lawns for up to five dollars a day.

Up from town, on spruce- and elm-shaded streets, the gabled homes survive, monuments to laissez faire and caveat emptor. Their temporary residents, the August visitors, breakfast on big sweet melons at the Reading Room (served by reverential Negroes with close-cropped white hair) before a round of golf at the "Spa" and a hot sulfur bath. No need to get to the races much before two.

In the Saratoga I know, the *Racing Form* outsells *The New York Times* two to one. Henry James once called it the "northernmost Southern city" and Jimmy Cannon, the sportswriter, dubbed it "the Coney Island of the underworld," an allusion to the days before the Kefauver hearings when gambling and prostitution were its main sources of income.

For a while after the gamblers were driven out of town, the Piping Rock, one of the fancier casinos, tried to make a go of it as a straight nightclub. But after a couple of summers it was burned down for insurance money, and now its charred remains are a fitting remembrance of an earlier era.

Thoroughbred racing first came to Saratoga in 1863 on the site of what is now a small training track called Horse Haven. When I was quite small, Horse Haven was the special place my father and I would go to ride together and, sometimes, to race each other on our ponies.

To get to Horse Haven we had to pass through a gate, guarded by a small, white-haired man, who would open it to let us through.

"Nice day, what-what?" my father would say to the man.

"Nice day, what-what?" I'd repeat to the man.

The white-haired man would give us a friendly wave and my father and I would laugh.

After only one year at Horse Haven, racing was moved across Union Avenue to its present location. There is no more pleasant racing in America than the twenty-four-day meeting held in front of a wooden grandstand little changed from the day the Travers, the oldest stakes race in the United States, was first run there in 1864.

In the infield stately elms form a lush parenthesis around a silver pond. Behind the grandstand, in the paddock, the horses walk in easy circles beneath the trees, scrutinized by their prospective backers. The trainers arrive to saddle them, just as the trainers arrived to saddle Upset the day he beat Man O'War in 1919. The owners bend to speak in confidential tones to the little men in bright silks who will enforce their instructions.

"Ri-ders *up!*" comes the cry. Mounted, the thoroughbred parade is led to the starting gate by outriders in pink coats, the colorful prelude to the minute-and-a-half scramble that punctuates the afternoon nine times each day.

It was not to the grandstand I used to go at all, but to the backstretch. It was a totally relaxed atmosphere where stable hands and wives and children spent sunny, lazy afternoons picnicking under the elms and watching the races.

Sometimes, if the race started on the backstretch, Mr. Cassidy, the starter, would take my cousin Judy and me with him up to the little green stand beside the gate. There he squeezed a buzzer that rang a bell and opened the doors of the starting gate. We got to know all the assistant starters—big, strong men in khaki shirts and pants who told endless stories about the war and the women they had loved. Between the races they swore and played poker inside the totalizator board.

Many days the best was saved for last. That was when my father would come to the backstretch early, before the last race had been run. He often did so, because he was usually bored sitting in the grandstand and would take the first opportunity to leave. A lot of trainers don't much like going to the races, where they have to wear suits and neckties and make pleasant conversation with the owners. They like horses, they like to see their horses run, they *love* to see their horses *win*. But if none of their horses is running, it can be pretty dull just sitting there day after day.

So along about the sixth race my father would often walk across the infield to the backstretch. He would walk down the shed to check on all his horses and chat for a little while with the grooms or with Mr. Mergler, his foreman.

Then he'd say "Let's go," and Judy and I would pile into

the back seat of his station wagon and roll the windows down. My father would drive right over next to the starting gate, lining up with it and facing in the same direction as the horses. When the horses broke from the gate at the start of the race, my father would step on the accelerator, and Judy and I would lean out the windows to watch the jockeys and listen to them yelling at each other, whipping and maneuvering for position. My father would drive the entire length of the backstretch on the little road that paralleled it, matching the horses' pace exactly. Once you have seen and *heard* a race in this way, watching it from a distance in the grandstand seems very pallid.

I had just turned seventeen my last summer in Saratoga. My father had a houseful with his second family, so it was decided I would stay with my grandfather, a proposal I liked.

My grandmother hadn't felt like making the trip that year and my grandfather was pleased to have companionship in the large room he had taken in the home of a Saratoga dentist. We were wonderfully companionable roommates. Mawkishly dependent on my grandmother when she was around to spoil him, pick up after him, and find his glasses for him, he was quite a different man in her absence. It was as if his independence, suppressed for however many months, was suddenly freed. (The trait had a curious antecedent: half a century before, my grandmother had stalled the Model T across a dusty railroad platform with a train rapidly approaching a quarter of a mile down the tracks. My grandmother, being neither fool nor heroine, grabbed my eight-year-old father and left my grandfather—who up to that moment had never driven an automobile—to fend for himself. Calmly, he moved to the driver's seat, turned over the ignition, and drove slowly off the tracks to where his wife and child were huddled on the other side. "Get in," he said, from behind the steering wheel. My grandfather drove from that moment on. My grandmother never drove again.)

Now I was my grandfather's chauffeur, getting up with him each morning at six, driving him to the stable, helping him with the horses' names, going with him to the rail of the training track while he clocked their workouts. We would come home around ten to a breakfast of melon and eggs, and I would feel a grown-up, satisfied kind of tired, full of the sense of accomplishment that comes from completing a day's work before noon.

After a nap, my grandfather would go devotedly to the races. I would drop him at the clubhouse and head for the more informal atmosphere of the backstretch. The usual backstretch attractions were augmented that summer by Maggie.

I'd known her for a long time, ever since she moved into a house near Simon's. (When Simon first saw Maggie's father, a jockey, he jumped on his bicycle, pedaled home, and told his mother: "There's a kid no bigger than me—he's got his own house and everything!") Maggie had always been a skinny tomboy. Now, suddenly, she had blossomed. By unspoken agreement we met on the backstretch each afternoon.

My grandfather went early to bed those summer evenings, while I read a book or, occasionally, went to the movies by myself. Restless one such evening, I called Maggie. Sure, she said, she'd love to go to a movie. There was even a suggestion in her voice of other possibilities.

In my grandfather's new Chrysler I headed to Saratoga Lake, where she was living that summer. The narrow, winding road around the lake dips and turns. I had just reached a hollow before a sharp bank when I realized that a car was speeding toward me in my lane. I swerved to miss it, but the road was too narrow. In the collision, about half head-on, I was thrown against the windshield. Neither I nor the young couple in the other car, who but a moment before had been petting and drinking beer, was any more than shaken up. My grandfather, when I called him, seemed calm. I said I could handle everything. There was no need to call my father.

It took about three hours to complete the agony of police paperwork and the arranging for tow trucks and body shops. My grandfather, worried about me, had called my father, who arrived shortly afterward at the police station. My father stayed masterfully under control. Only when he had at last been released by the police did I realize the extent of his rage, hidden just beneath the surface. Now it exploded. I had betrayed my grandfather. I had gambled with his health. What if he had had a heart attack while I was off "seeing some girl"? Why was it that everything I touched turned to disaster? I was just lucky that the shock had not killed my grandfather.

Neither tire skids, the police report, nor my protestations would satisfy him. One moment he was angry because I had taken the car, the next because I had wrecked it. He berated me the long drive home, his voice shaking with rage.

I fought back tears, trying to absorb his wrath without going to pieces. Exhausted, afraid, not knowing what to say, I said nothing, staring out into the night. He mistook my expression for one of cynicism. Suddenly he reached across the car seat and grabbed my shoulder, squeezing it, shaking me, more furious than I had ever seen him.

"How dare you just sit there waiting for me to finish!" he shouted. "Why, you punk . . ." I don't remember what he said after that.

The next day he told me he was going to sell *my* car, the 1957 Ford convertible he had given me, quite unexpectedly, only a month before. A week later he said he had visited Williams College, where I wanted to go. He was forbidding me to apply.

"But why?" I asked, incredulous.

He said he had looked into it. He had learned that it was a "snob school." That was all. It might be fine for others but I had been spoiled enough. He didn't want to discuss it any further. No matter how unfair it might seem, he said, someday I would be grateful.

I felt like I had been struck with a timber. My hands and feet went numb. Every pore seemed contorted by the injustice. I thought of Johnny Tremaine, Joan of Arc, Thomas à Becket, now comrades in adversity. If that's the way you want it, I thought to myself, I can play that game too. I'll quit school. I'll join the Marines. Then when I get out I'll go where I damn well please.

Then I calmed down. My going into the Marines would only please him and punish me, I realized. The next week he softened. He bought me a motorcycle. I damn near froze my ass riding it all over Baltimore my senior year at McDonogh.

That last year—1959—I found myself dealing with new and disturbing things: ideas. I suppose my introduction to them came from reading a fictionalized account of the 1924 kidnapping and "thrill killing" of Bobby Franks, an eight-year-old Chicago youth, by two college students, Nathan Leopold and Richard Loeb. Rich, bright, with everything going for them, Leopold and Loeb had coldly and clinically stalked, kidnapped, and murdered the Franks boy. Not for any motive except to "test" the Nietzschean concept that some men were above law and other conventions of society. These two "supermen" had been caught because Nathan Leopold had left his glasses at the scene of the murder. The story became only richer when Clarence Darrow came out of retirement to plead their cause in a court of law. His defense summation lasted three days and ended in a brilliant peroration against capital punishment: "I am pleading for the future, for a time when hatred and cruelty will not control the hearts of men, when we can learn that all life is worth saving, and that mercy is the highest attribute of man."

I read *The Amazing Crime and Trial of Leopold and Loeb.* I read *Clarence Darrow for the Defense.* And I took a bus twelve miles into Baltimore to buy the newly published autobiography of Joliet Penitentiary inmate Nathan Leopold, *Life Plus Ninety-nine Years.* I combed the school library for magazine articles about the case and reviews of the books I had read. I became intrigued with law and psychology. I took to railing against capital punishment and on vacation in Miami that Christmas I got to talking about the case with a friend's father, a criminal attorney and former county prosecutor. I felt certain that any lawyer would feel as I did about Darrow's brilliance and the just disposition of the Leopold-Loeb case. I also thought that Leopold's work in creating an interprison correspondence school and in volunteering his body for medical experiments made a powerful testament to rehabilitation. But my friend's father did not agree. He said that the two kidnappers should have been executed. He said the country would be much better off if capital punishment were more widespread.

When I returned to school, I set out to challenge the arguments that my friend's father had made. During off-hours and on weekends I labored fiercely over a long essay, a brief against capital punishment. "Whereas in the past," I wrote with what I intended as legal flourish, "society sought revenge and affixed blame erroneously on the criminal alone, it has been learned that environmental conflict and lack of guidance, to list but two of literally thousands of factors that mold an individual's personality, are the real causes for the crime."

From the consideration of capital punishment and criminal rehabilitation, my mind moved cautiously to larger, more abstract questions: man's purpose on earth, the value of goals. In painful sessions with my typewriter, I tried to work my way through ideas that, though beyond my control, made fewer demands upon me once they were set down on paper. More often than not, these groping essays would barely outline the problem: What is success? How can one be completely honest? Is there a God?

Understandably, for one in uniform, the idea of conformity was much on my mind. "With the rise of the 'beatnik,' " I wrote, "the conformist has been cast as an ignoble creature.

He has appeared dull and without a mind of his own. But, except for a few ascetics with a single goal so eminent [sic] that they are willing to face the wave of society against them, we are all conformists to one extent or another. There is nothing wrong with this; it is natural. The conformist can think, can have ideals, convictions. He may lead a rich, full, natural, and rewarding life.''

Obviously, I was trying to say that just because I looked like everybody else didn't mean I wasn't also unique: "Slovenly dress, poetry recitation, and phony philosophy may be the symbols of the *physical* nonconformist. But the true nonconformist may be a churchgoing, Lion-clubbing businessman, banker, architect, teacher, or what-have-you, as long as his thinking is not regimented by conformity.''

Having solved that one, I rested easier. But soon an even more foreboding notion took hold of me. I began to think that perhaps I, alone among men, could push back the frontiers of man's knowledge, could think thoughts heretofore unthought in all of civilization. My relief at having worked out the conformity question was nothing next to an almost suffocating sense of obligation: that I had been chosen to explore, alone, the human condition.

In a long, rambling, and disorganized treatise that I called "The Thoughts of Jasper,'' I described the nature of my newly discovered curse: "Jasper craves to be equal rather than superior, and to enjoy the simple things of life. Yet he feels he is superior and therefore he has to use his mind toward understanding the abstractions of life.'' And then the kicker: "But Jasper is a human being and as such succumbs to all the natural instincts and cravings of his body.'' My dilemma, in short: How do you go about becoming a seventeen-year-old philosopher-king when thoughts of screwing keep interrupting your reveries about the nature of man?

Perhaps the first realization I had that I was not all that alone came when I submitted one of my essays to the school paper for publication. I was astounded when the faculty adviser to the paper had a ready title for my upbeat assertions: "Carpe Diem." My surprise in discovering a catch phrase for my insights gave way to a kind of relief: perhaps the obligation to unravel the mysteries of life was not singly mine after all.

One effect of my thinking was the erosion of what until then had been a kind of Sunday-school faith in God. Now I was becoming a rationalist. Religion began to appear *irrational*. What kind of omniscient wisdom would insist that heaven was the reward only of those who believed in God's son? What about all those who had never heard of God's son? And what kind of sense did it make that a christened baby got a better shake in heaven than an unchristened one?

I began to seek an absolute: something to resolve ethical contradictions. From a diary: "I am baffled by the conflict of codes—moral, religious, legal, medical, etc. What is wrong by one code is not by another. One can run a stop sign and be safe morally, religiously, and medically, but pinched legally. Yet the judge doesn't care if the Catholic eats meat on Friday or if the taxpayer brushes his teeth. But send that same unbrushed taxpayer to a dentist and wham, a sermon." For a while I thought I had found an expedient guide in the concept of pure honesty. But the more I probed and experimented with the idea, the less workable it became. Not everyone, I quickly discovered, was ready for pure honesty.

I returned to a state of uncertainty. In an editorial for the school paper I tried to define it:

> I am an American. I have been taught about the equality of man; I am confronted by religious and racial prejudices. I have been told of the integrity and the benevolent intentions of politicians. I have read of corruption and vicuna coats. I have read of the ideals of democracy, freedom, and equality; my newspaper is filled with Little Rock and synagogue bombings. My bible says it is a sin to kill; I study the history of World War II. I am confronted by the frowns of people who use phrases like

"the scourge of juvenile delinquency." I read the praise of youth groups. I am told that man is sacred; I study him as an animal. I read of Adam and Eve; I study evolution.

I am confused. I see, hear, and read of undisputed principles; I see, hear, and read of contrary practices. I am led to individualism and encouraged to think freely; I am crushed by conformity and warned that "things without remedy should be without regard. . . ."

I read and hear of the evils of *other* societies, *other* nations, *other* religions, and *other* creeds. Why am *I* so fortunate?

I hear of atomic fall-out, of the growing world population, of an imminent war, of a coming depression. Where does it all lead?

A loved one dies. Death I cannot understand.

I am scared; I am faced by decisions which will mold my life. I wonder about the purpose of man; I wonder about the meaning of success. My sense of values is ever-changing; my goals in life vary from day to day. To whom am I indebted? Myself? My fellow man? Some undefinable power?

I am protected in the world as it swirls along. But soon I must leap into it. Am I ready? Where will I land? What will I be? Where will I go? What should I expect from this world? To what must I dedicate myself?

I am confused. What kind of world am I living in whose preaching and actions differ?

Who am I? What course must I follow? The one of least resistance; or a bolder course leading perhaps to misery?

I do not know the answer to so many questions.

I am an adolescent.

The essay was well received. The school chaplain devoted his sermon to it the next Sunday. Another school newspaper wrote for permission to reprint it. Though I did not resolve any of the dilemmas, I enjoyed the attention and praise I got for having expressed them. And after a while that came to be more important than resolving the conflicts.

Mr. Kinard, the English teacher, was called "Bobo the dog-faced boy" because he looked like a basset hound. But a boy he was not—had not been since he left South Carolina to get his master's degree in English literature at Columbia University nearly half a century before.

He had not lost his resonant South Carolina inflections; perhaps they had even deepened as he recollected his origins in the tranquility of the Maryland hills and advancing age. "Kay-ree," he would ask me, rhetorically, "if Shakespeare had never written a single play, why would we remember him? That's right, Kay-ree, foah his in-*comp*-arable poetry."

The only way I could get out of a test he was giving one afternoon—I was unprepared—was to be interviewed by the visiting Columbia recruiter. We got along well and he all but assured me that if I applied I would be accepted. So I applied to Columbia, along with Stanford (my first choice), Berkeley, Northwestern, and Rutgers. I did not apply to Harvard, Princeton, or Yale because I was certain I would not be accepted. I was turned down by Stanford and Berkeley and had no real desire to go to Rutgers. That left Columbia and Northwestern. I asked Mr. Kinard what he thought. He said but two words: "Kay-ree, Columbia."

I expected another row with my father when I told him that I wanted to go to Columbia. If Williams's reputation as a snob school had bothered him, what of Columbia's as a "pinko" school, a cradle of sedition, even communism?

I decided to break the news in a letter. He answered, to my surprise, that he was delighted. It took me some time to understand his attitude. Finally I realized that Columbia's radical reputation had not reached my father. To him, it was that fine school that had turned out his good friends "Maj" Odum, a horse trainer, and Jimmy Kilroe, the California racing secretary.

It had been a long time since Mr. Kinard had been to Columbia. But he had kept up with the school as best he could. He was eager for more information. "When you get there, Kay-ree, I want you to find out about a Mr. Lionel Trilling. Mr. Trilling is a very interesting man. He's just had some things, shocking things, to say about Mr. Robert Frost. Will you do that for me, Kay-ree? I expect a report on Mr. Trilling.''

I said that I most certainly would.

My mother drove up from Miami for my graduation. My grandparents drove down from New York. My father was going to fly in from Los Angeles. Then at the last minute, he couldn't get away. He had to run a horse at Santa Anita. He said he knew I'd understand.

I was nervous about graduation because I hoped to win an award—a silver cup—for creative writing. It would be the first presentation of the Eustace S. Glascock award—named after the author of "The McDonogh Uniform."

> A McDonogh suit, for your son to wear?
> Ah! Madam, they're not for sale.
> And he who dons must never doff—
> As a nun who takes the veil.
>
> The dirt and the grime of strife and of toil
> Only brighten its marvelous hue;
> But the shiftless shame of an idle life
> Will rot it through and through.
>
> Yet we have no weaver of magical skill.
> Our tailor's no Fairyland elf.
> We've merely discovered that to wear such a suit
> The wearer must make it himself. . . .

When, a couple of months before graduation, the headmaster had announced the new award, the school paper had been besieged with poetry. I even knocked out a few iambs myself. But then, the award wasn't just for poetry but for *creative* writing.

When they announced my name as the first recipient of the

Eustace S. Glascock award, I thought seriously of crying. Then I thought better of it.

My friend Jamie, a soft-featured cherub who played the trombone, and I were planning to spend the summer hitchhiking to California and back.

Jamie's girlfriend, Harmony, lived in Louisville, Kentucky. That's where he wanted to head for. That was okay with me. For three years at school I had listened to Jamie tell stories about his girl and the things they used to do together. What she liked best, Jamie used to tell us, was to lean over him until his nose rested in the space between her breasts. Then she'd shimmy her whole upper torso, pummeling him into ecstacy. No, I wouldn't mind going west by way of Louisville at all.

We made it to Louisville in three rides on the second day. We stayed at Jamie's girlfriend's house. We had the place to ourselves. Jamie's girl and her brother and father spent most of the day at the hospital, where Harmony's mother was having both breasts removed because of cancer.

The next day, hitchhiking through Tennessee on our way to Mobile, where Jamie had relatives, we were stranded for four hours. As night fell, we heard a train not too far from the highway. We decided to try to hop a freight.

In less than half an hour a coal freight chugged slowly by. It wasn't very hard, even with our heavy duffel bags slung over our shoulders, to run alongside, take hold of the ladder, and swing ourselves onto it. We climbed the ladder and looked over into a dark abyss. We tossed our duffel bags down to the inside and listened for the reassuring thud. When it came, we let our feet hang toward the bottom of the car, then slowly, carefully, pushed off to land without injury in the well of the car.

The bottom was not flat. In fact, it was quite steep. We had no sooner congratulated ourselves on our feat when I turned to ask Jamie what kind of car he thought this was.

"Coal," he answered.

"Yeah, that's what I think too," I said. "Listen, I think we may be in trouble."

"Yeah?"

"Well, I can only think of three reasons why this car doesn't have a flat bottom."

"I'm listening."

"First, the bottom opens up to let the coal out."

"Second?"

"Second, the whole car tips up to let the coal out."

"Never mind the third," said Jamie. "Let's get outta here."

We managed to jump off the moving train without hurting ourselves. But it was a long wait till the next one. We were tired and dirty. And, when it came, the next train was barreling along.

We ran. We ran until we thought we couldn't run any more. Finally, with heroic effort, Jamie swung an arm and a leg onto a ladder that led down from one of the cars. He pulled himself onto it. I kept running alongside, stumbling over the ties. I was about to give up when Jamie reached out for me and grabbed me by the arm and shirt. At the same time I reached for the ladder, clutched it, and with Jamie's help hung onto it. We rested there for a time, panting to catch our breath. Again we pulled ourselves to the top of the car and threw our duffel bags into the dark interior. This time the car was flat-bottomed. We took our sleeping bags out of our duffels and inflated our air mattresses. We settled down for a long ride. No sooner had we gotten settled than we noticed that the train seemed to be slowing down. In a little while we were certain. It had slowed to a walking pace. Then it stopped altogether.

We climbed the sides of the car and peeked over the edge. What we saw looked like a huge parking lot for trains. The yard was totally deserted. Then we remembered the date: the third of July. The train, we realized, was parked for the holiday weekend.

We trekked back to the highway, a mile or so away, and

bedded down for the night. We got a ride the next morning but it still took us another day and night to reach Mobile.

In Mobile we stayed with Jamie's aunt and uncle, who kept feeding us grits (which I liked, but not three times a day). As soon as we could, without offending Jamie's aunt and uncle, we got going again. It was too damned hot in Mobile. The local joke was that the temperature was "over a hundred in the shade but there ain't no shade." We laughed only the first few times we heard it.

In New Orleans, our next stop, Jamie took me to my first strip show. And my second. And my third. Jamie was an aficionado; he couldn't get enough. I was horny enough already. I saw no point in paying good money just to be made more miserable.

We spent what seemed like weeks hitchhiking across Texas to San Antonio, where Jamie had more relatives. We learned to sleep anywhere. A fellow, tired or just looking for conversation, would pick us up. We'd thank him, ask where he was headed, tell him where to let us out, make ourselves comfortable, and fall asleep.

Outside of Pecos, Texas, a dismal, dusty place where we were stranded for three hours, a free-lance oil worker, or "roughneck," picked us up. He was drunk, so Jamie took over the wheel. While the roughneck swigged vile whiskey out of a bottle, we pretended to join him. When he said "I don't care, anywhere you boys wanna go," we took him a couple of hundred miles out of his way and left him sleeping it off by the side of the road.

In San Antonio we saw the Alamo, ate Mexican food, and walked along the San Antonio river. In Carlsbad, New Mexico, we saw the caverns and the fifty thousand bats that fly out of them at night. In Albuquerque we dug down deep into our duffels to find the two most wrinkled cord suits in North America. Wearing them, we crashed a square dance. Somehow I wound up necking with the queen of the rodeo.

We were broke and wondering what we were going to do in Sante Fe when we were picked up by four girls who had just graduated from a Connecticut junior college. Their station wagon was bulging with camping gear, suitcases, hairnets, crackers, and cheese. They said they needed a little help loading and unloading the car and setting up their tents at campsites. We told them we needed some help too: food, shelter, companionship, transportation. We would spend ten days together.

We sang songs and told stories, clean and dirty. We held hands and cooked hamburgers on the little outdoor grills which the national park campsites provided. As a joke one night the six of us went into a diner. While we ordered Cokes, Jamie went into the men's room. When he came out, brushing his teeth and wearing only a towel around his waist, I snapped his picture and everybody in the place turned to stare and to laugh.

At Bryce Canyon we paired off—Jamie with Ginny, the best looking; me with Linda, the smartest—leaving the other two girls with each other.

The Grand Canyon: I don't know whose idea it was to choose the experienced hiker's trail as our route to the bottom. But of course we all agreed to it. We were so anxious to get an early start that we skimped on breakfast. And Ginny had read somewhere that hikers should eat light.

We practically skipped down the seven miles to the bottom. Even with lots of stops to take in the incredible beauty, we made it by early afternoon to the Ghost Ranch, where we swam in a natural spring-fed pool at the bottom of the canyon.

It was after two when Ginny suggested we'd better get going, that we had a long climb ahead of us. Hungry now, we were all quick to agree. We filled our canteens and headed out.

After two or three miles uphill in suffocating, dry heat—our canteens empty, our legs aching, our feet beginning to blister, our stomachs growling—we realized we were in for trouble.

Gloria began to cry. She said she couldn't go any further. Marta took her shoes off. We began to spread out over half a mile or so, each of us maintaining whatever pace we could. I was surprised to see Ginny and Linda ahead of Jamie and me. I couldn't understand the source of their strength and energy. I marveled at their strides. Without their example, I thought, surely I would give up. The thought of potential humiliation helped to keep me going.

In another hour, with the sun mercifully beginning to descend to the canyon rim, we came upon a running spring surrounded by lush blackberry bushes. Ginny and Linda, having already gorged themselves, were lying on the grass resting when Jamie and I arrived. Our faces in the water, we slurped shamelessly until we had to come up for air. We tore our hands with thorns as we stuffed our mouths with blackberries. We lay down beside Linda and Ginny on the grass.

After an hour, joined now by Gloria and Marta, we packed up again and started out. The rim of the canyon still loomed miles above us. Within another hour we were as miserable as before. We stopped to rest, establishing a pattern that would continue throughout our long and painful night: walk an hour, rest half an hour. Once I stopped and lay down in the middle of the path. I didn't even move when Jamie told me that my head was resting on a mound of donkey manure.

We reached the top at dawn. No one spoke. We went to our sleeping bags and slept all day. That night we got up and silently went to dinner at a coffee shop. Then we went back to sleep. The next day we ached all over.

Nobody sang or even talked very much on the drive to Las Vegas. Once there, the girls checked into a motel that Jamie and I could not afford. We found a small trailer that a fellow said he'd let us sleep in for two dollars. The girls picked us up around six and we quickly discovered Las Vegas's chief virtue: we could go from club to club watching the lounge shows for free, courtesy of all the slot machine players who subsidized the entertainment. We saw my old favorite, Frankie Laine, sing all his old favorites. And Sophie Tucker did what she had done for the previous half-century. The tab for the evening was the quarter I lost in the slot machine, just to say I had gambled. At two in the morning the six of us had hamburgers at the Sands Coffee Shop. Shirley MacLaine and her husband sat at the next table. It seemed exciting at the time.

I didn't want to push our luck. I felt we had done Las Vegas just right and wanted to head on to California the next morning. No, the girls said, the motel had a pool and they wanted to relax by it for a day or two more. Jamie seemed uncertain what he wanted to do. I argued that it had been so successful a day that we ought to leave before anything happened to spoil our memories of what I instinctively felt was a rather unsavory place.

We returned to find our trailer had been broken into. Jamie's electric shaver and a portable radio we had picked up at a Mobile pawnshop were missing. And one of the beds appeared to have been used as a trampoline.

In the morning we told the owner what had happened. He was supremely unsympathetic.

"You've got some nerve complaining," he said. "Who told you it was okay to bring a girl in there?"

"Girl," we said. "What girl?"

"That girl you humped in there last night. I oughta charge you extra."

We started to explain that we hadn't brought any girl in but his expression indicated an unwillingness to believe us. So we said okay, have it your way.

The experience convinced Jamie that we ought to get going. We took our leave of the girls with very mixed feelings. We promised to write each other and to get together again in the fall.

We got lucky on the highway: an air-conditioned Cadillac

whisked us serenely through the 115-degree heat of Death Valley. We were just passing through San Bernardino when the radio reported the arrest, an hour earlier, of Doctor Bernard Finch and his office assistant, Carol Tregoff, for the murder of Mrs. Finch.

When we got to Los Angeles, I called my father. No answer. We headed for the Santa Anita racetrack, where I was certain we could find beds.

Santa Anita was deserted. Too late, I realized that racing—and with it all the stables—had moved to Hollywood Park. There seemed no alternative but to climb over the fence and sleep on our air mattresses.

Jamie and I were awakened by seven or eight cop cars that converged around us. We came out with our hands up.

At the police station I called my stepmother and learned that my father had flown to New York the day before to be with my grandfather, who had taken ill. It seemed ironic. Here we'd been on the road nearly six weeks and had finally reached Los Angeles, only to find out my father was in New York. It had taken him less than six hours to get there.

It was just an unfortunate misunderstanding, we told the police. We didn't mean any harm. The police looked dubious but even they finally agreed there was no need to make a federal case out of it.

Racing had actually moved to Del Mar. When my father returned from New York the next day, the three of us drove to Del Mar. He fixed us up in a wooden shack not much bigger than an outhouse, one of hundreds built for stable help. We weren't complaining. It had a roof, a table, and two chairs. We swept it out and thought it was a palace.

With my father's help, we were able to land jobs with a horse auction company. The sales barns were filling up for a yearling auction two weeks away. Jamie and I were put to work "mucking out" some forty stalls a day, at fifty cents a stall. On the night of the sale, resplendent in rented tuxedos, Jamie and I served as ushers and as "spotters"—assisting the auctioneer in spotting timid bidders. A lot of Hollywood celebrities came to the sale. Ronald Reagan, whose acting career had dwindled to "Death Valley Days," tipped me a dollar for seating him. Johnny Cash, a surly man, sulked because his seat was too far from ringside. Lawrence Welk bid unsuccessfully on three different horses.

"Well-l-l," the auctioneer would begin his spiel as a skittish colt or filly tiptoed around the ring. "Who'll give ten thousand to start? I got five, six, seven. All righty, nowya, who'll give ten thousand fora, who'll bid ten thousand dolla billa, billya, willya, willya . . ."

I'd look at Lawrence Welk or some of the other bidders in my section. If they gave me the slightest nod, or a wink, I'd yell "Yooooo" nearly as loud as I could. Jamie and I made fifty dollars apiece for the night's work, and I was convinced there was nothing to making money.

The next night, to celebrate, we went to Tijuana in an old rattletrap we borrowed from one of the grooms, staking him ten bucks for the car and for not saying anything about it to my father.

Jamie and I left suddenly one Sunday. My father was visiting his family about twenty miles up the road and we were sitting around the stable, bored, facing another corn flakes dinner, when we decided it was time to go. If the rides hit right, we would be able to stop and say good-by to my father on our way north.

Jamie told me he didn't mind stopping, even though the fellow who had picked us up was going all the way to Los Angeles.

"Never mind," I said. "I'll call him on the telephone."

My father seemed to understand. I told myself that he and I took a certain pride in not getting sentimental about things. That's why he hadn't come to my graduation. That's why I ignored his birthday. We just didn't go in for that sort of thing. It only bothered me for a week or so.

Outside of LA we got a ride in a big truck and took turns sleeping on a narrow mattress in the cab behind the driver. By the time morning came we were only about twenty miles south of San Francisco.

That was when we got the idea to buy a car. We went to a dealer and found a presentable-looking heap that he'd let us have for fifty dollars. He needed the room on the lot, he said. That was the only reason he'd let it go so cheaply. We drove it around the block and it seemed okay. Out on the road we stopped and got some cooking equipment and some plates and silverware so that we could buy food and camp out across the country on the way back.

About ten miles from San Francisco the car started smoking badly. We dubbed it "Lord Chesterfield," which we thought clever. By the time we hit the city proper, it was coughing as well as smoking. It expired at the crest of the San Francisco Bay Bridge. Jamie had to get out and push it the last few feet before gravity took over. We coasted into the naval base at Treasure Island. There we conned a sailor into taking it off our hands for ten dollars. Then he conned us into agreeing to let him send us the money.

Fifty dollars poorer, we checked into a cheap hotel. We went to one of those places that feature pitchers of beer, banjo music, and singing. We had about three pitchers between us and I had to open the cab door on the way back to the hotel to throw up in the street. Jamie was sick too, but I was the one who couldn't get out of bed for another full day and night.

By the time we left San Francisco all we wanted to do was get home. We made it halfway across the country in two days of steady thumbing. We had spent a summer together and now, almost home, we had our first bad argument. I don't even remember what it was about. But the upshot was that we went on alone. "Screw you," I said. "I'll make better time on my own."

I realized the hardheadedness of my action as soon as I

saw Jamie ride off. He turned to ask if I wanted to come along just before he got in the car. I did want to. I knew I was being stupid and willful, but I waved him on.

I had waited for a ride for nearly an hour when I heard a train whistle. What the hell, I said to myself. Why not? It's not the fourth of July.

I hopped a freight and rode it into a big yard in Omaha about three hours away. When it came to a stop, I got off and walked down to a cluster of trainmen having coffee. I took a chance and told them what I was up to. They directed me to a more-than-hundred-car freight that was leaving for Chicago in about an hour. The best place to ride, they said, was on any one of the flatcars carrying a refrigerated truck van. The van would be my roof. They even told me where I could get coffee and a sandwich.

I ate my hundredth greasy hamburger of the trip and made my way back to find a hospitable flatcar. On it, I pulled my sleeping bag out of the duffel and lay down, using it as mattress and pillow. In a little while I heard the rumble of the engine and, way down the tracks, the first of a series of loud crashes as one car, then another, came into contact with the one behind it. A cadence developed—bam, bam, Bam, BAM! BAM!!!—until finally my car was in motion with a jolt that all but threw me into the air. Then the sound began to recede—BAM!!! BAM! Bam, bam, bam—until the train began to move in the other direction. In a little while the cycle would begin again. It went on for hours. It was dark when the train finally pulled out.

About two in the morning intense cramps forced me into a fetal position. The train was clacking down the tracks at a brisk pace and I didn't know what I was going to do. Then, suddenly, I had no choice. I pulled my pants down and took hold of one of the struts above me on the truck van. I stuck my buttocks out as far over the side of the train as I could and let go my bowels. The wind swirled the fetid spray into my hair and clothes and eyes. When I was done, I wiped myself dry as best I could with my undershirt. Then I threw it into a passing cornfield.

Through the long next day I rode through flatlands filled with corn and wheat and barley. I lay motionless on the flatcar, hot and dusty. I was thirsty more than I was hungry, and I wondered if the train would ever stop.

It was nearly four in the afternoon when it did, pulling into an enormous freight yard that might have been anywhere in the Midwest to judge from the open, rolling plains that surrounded it. Getting off the train, I was as tired and dirty as I could ever remember being.

The only thing in sight was a factory, about a mile away. It turned out to be some sort of processing plant. When I walked inside, all the workers stopped what they were doing to stare at me. I asked someone where the men's room was, and he pointed. When I looked in the mirror I didn't recognize myself. My skin was as dark as earth.

After I had cleaned up, the man who had directed me to the washroom told me that I was about twelve miles from Chicago. He told me where to find the highway and how to get to O'Hare Airport. I took the first flight back to New York.

That fall I read *On the Road,* which described Kerouac's cross-country adventures with his friend Paul Moriarity. I wondered what all the fuss was about. Usually the narrator gave up hitchhiking after a few hours and wound up on a Greyhound bus. I had kept a journal of *our* trip and decided that I too could write a novel about it. I had the title—*Around the States in Eighty Rides*—which is just what it took us, not counting the plane from Chicago to New York. But the first thing I would learn at Columbia was that, the Eustace S. Glascock award notwithstanding, I didn't know the first thing about writing.

V

In the fall of 1959, I took with me to Columbia a wardrobe trunk, three advance credits in English, and expectations of college formed mainly from watching Robert Cummings and Betty Grable cavorting in matching cardigan letter sweaters. I was not burdened by compulsive curiosity. I brought with me no childhood yearnings to become a doctor, lawyer, or financier. I was perfectly willing to leave the excitement of pushing back new frontiers in science to others. And yet my appetites were large. I sought nothing less than the college experience.

Freshman week conformed quite nicely to my preconceptions. I actually liked the supposed indignity of having to wear a beanie. I liked the welcoming speeches, rich in their vocabulary of promise, redolent with phrases about Columbia men and their "rightful place" as "leaders of the free world." I liked the evening in John Jay Hall that began with an impressively casual sophomore greeting us as "fellow Harvard rejects" (robust laughter), followed by his imparting to us the "secret" of a successful Columbia career: to wit, if we forgot to change trains at 96th Street on our way to Columbia's 116th Street subway stop, and thus found ourselves at the 116th Street stop on the *express* line, we should "go back to 96th and take the local. To walk through Morningside Park is suicide" (nervous laughter).

I particularly liked being led, over pitchers of beer, through a medley of Columbia's fight songs, ending with a rousing version of "Who Owns New York?":

> Oh, who owns New York? Oh, who owns New York?
> Oh, who owns New York? the people say.
> Why, we own New York. Yes, we own New York.
> C-O-L-U-M-B-I-A!

I was surprised the next morning when a number of my new classmates called the evening a waste of time. (I had also been disappointed by their insistence that wearing beanies was childishly absurd.) I dismissed them as incurable cynics.

The evening before the Columbia-Princeton game I took a bus south into New Jersey farmland. The football game was a good excuse to see two friends from McDonogh and to congratulate each other on joining the Ivy League.

The very idea of Princeton had been dancing in my psyche ever since an evening, years before at the Bath Club in Miami, when I had been entertained by Princeton's singing group, the Tigertones. It had been my first exposure to the buttondown, tweed-coated, smooth-haired Ivy League style. One look and I wanted to burn my boxy, broad-shouldered sports jacket, my pink slacks, and my thin, blue suede belt (buckled, ever so stylishly, on the hip). I didn't know how it was acquired, but whatever it was that the Tigertones had, I wanted it.

Now, visiting at Princeton, I realized I wanted it more than ever. My enthusiasm for Columbia paled as I contrasted Princeton's bucolic, manicured campus with ugly, urban Columbia. Princeton looked the way college was supposed to:

trees and fields instead of cement and slums, a citizenry that appeared to have been outfitted to a man at Brooks Brothers instead of the derelicts and the defeated who mingled with Columbia students on upper Broadway. And Princeton's students—so healthy looking, so well groomed, so reeking of insouciance. They *all* looked like Tigertones.

I watched enviously as what must have been nearly the entire town turned out for a victory eve bonfire and pep rally. At the game the next day I sat guiltily with my friends on the Princeton side, feeling ever more disloyal as the Columbia Lions took their traditional trouncing.

What little comfort I took from the weekend came from learning that weekly chapel attendance was mandatory for Princeton freshmen. On the bus back to New York I concentrated on that anachronism and reached the Port Authority terminal resolved to make the best of things.

Almost at once I found myself in trouble. I had bought into a chain letter at Princeton, paying some thirty-two dollars for the privilege. The payment took the form of two twenty-five-dollar savings bonds, which the seller immediately sent off to the two top names on a list in the letter. As instructed, I had retyped the letter in duplicate, deleting the top name on the ten-name list and adding mine to the bottom. As the procedure was repeated, the laws of geometric progression would take over, and when my name reached the top of the list I would receive some 5,696 savings bonds with a face value of $142,400. Not bad, I thought, for my first semester.

But the laws of human nature took over instead. Because the banks were closed that Sunday night, I made the mistake of accepting payment from my roommates in cash instead of savings bonds ("We can get those tomorrow"). Within three hours the letter had swept through the dorm like a brush fire; nearly three hundred freshmen had bought into it. All transactions had been in cash, and the idea of the savings bonds had gotten lost along the way. Someone had discovered that by making ten copies instead of two, it was possible to hustle up about $150 in fast-talking profit. Nobody at Columbia ever got a savings bond in the mail.

What I got, the following day, was a call from the Dean. He said he had traced the origins of the chain letter to me.

"Not . . . very . . .smart," he began when I came to see him. "Not even . . . very . . . original. My mother-in-law started a chain letter at Vassar. And that was in the twenties."

I nodded glumly, uncertain whether I was supposed to express admiration for his mother-in-law's precocity or chagrin for having been forty years behind the times. The dean said that I had not chosen an accepted method for making a name for myself at Columbia. He said he was putting "a tissue" in my file. I was not on formal probation but he would be following my progress with great interest. "We shall see what we shall see," he added, cryptically.

Having escaped such a close brush with disaster, I re-resolved to make the best of things. I went out for freshman crew, dutifully riding the subway for forty minutes each afternoon after classes to dip oars into used condoms and other urban flotsam on the Harlem River until my arms begged me to stop. I signed up to write for *Jester,* the college humor magazine, and spent several evenings staring at my typewriter before arriving reluctantly at the conclusion that I wasn't ready to be funny, just yet. And when a rally was organized in support of Charles Van Doren, the professor who with much furrowing of brow had won so much money on a television quiz program called "Twenty One"—a program that Americans were just learning had been rigged all along—I joined a cheering throng in support of the unfortunate teacher, until some cynic from a dorm window above us drowned out the rally with relentless basso profundo sighs on his tuba.

Even so, there was more support for Van Doren than for the Columbia Lions, who had lost their first five games. Bad enough that they had lost. What bothered me more was that nobody seemed to care. Bad enough that almost no one showed up for pep rallies; worse that so many of my classmates thought such apathy healthy. Columbia might belong to the Ivy League football conference, but Ivy—I could no longer deny—it wasn't.

I desperately needed something to be chauvinistic about. It was then that I discovered "the Hall," St. Anthony Hall—Columbia's most exclusive fraternity, peopled almost to a brother with very reasonable facsimiles of Tigertones. I quit crew. I forgot about *Jester*. I had found what I was looking for.

The Hall was unique among Columbia's nearly two dozen fraternities in a number of respects. While the others occupied converted apartment buildings on 113th and 114th streets, the Hall reposed in a splendid brownstone on Riverside Drive. While the rest of the houses drew their membership only from Columbia College, the Hall pledged from the university at large. It eschewed its Greek letters and cultivated a mystique that derived only in part from its rumored designation as a "secret society." No one outside its membership was supposed to know its leaders, or even their titles, and there were rumors of other "secrets" as well. In addition to the men who defined its flavor, the Hall boasted a substantial international contingent: two Greeks, an Irishman, a Swede, a German, and a trio of representatives from South America, each richer than the other and all, it was assumed, destined to become *presidentes* of their respective countries a few revolutions down the road.

That year the Hall was desperate for new members. Its very exclusivity had all but done it in. Suddenly it had found itself very nearly broke. The most expedient way to get money was to pledge a lot of new members. The goal was at least twenty.

I was one of the first to be invited for a "rush" lunch. When he had heard I was going to Columbia, my father's friend and St. A alumnus, Jimmy Kilroe, had written a letter to the rushing committee. With that first lunch, I knew which fraternity I wanted to join. (It never occurred to me not to join *any*.)

After two weeks of lunches, dinners, and cocktail parties; after giving all the brothers ample opportunity to observe whether or not we rushees wore white socks or violated such other rules of decorum as might prove embarrassing should we be so fortunate as to join the flock; and after according to each brother the proper measure of deferential reverence, Bert Evans, a laconic trucker's son from John O'Hara's coal-country hometown, took me aside one afternoon and told me I had nothing to worry about. He sealed his assurance with a wink.

And sure enough the next day those of us who had been invited once again to lunch were told that we lucky few, we eighteen, should feel mighty proud of ourselves, just as proud as they felt of us because, yes, we were now pledges.

It *was* a happy moment for me. I had wanted it and gotten it. But my satisfaction was short-lived. There was, after all, the Weintraub matter. Weintraub was a popular sophomore who had made a number of appearances at rushing functions at the Hall. He was engaging, with a big, wide smile and a laugh that came easily, almost no matter what one said to encourage it. And then, suddenly, nobody saw him any more. The question arose among those of us still rushing as to why he had stopped coming around. Was it on his own initiative, or was it because he was a Jew?

I went immediately to Bert, who we had concluded was in charge. I told him that we were upset about Weintraub. "He's a damned good guy," I said, "as well qualified as any of the rest of us. We think he's been blackballed because he's a Jew. I'm sorry to say this, but we're all ready to resign if Weintraub doesn't get in." I said that none of us wanted to belong to a "restricted" fraternity. Bert said to calm down, he would look into it.

About three nights later I was fast asleep in my motel-like room in "New" Hall when I felt someone shaking me.

"Get dressed," said a voice through my dream.

"What?" I woke up.

"Get dressed. You're being initiated."

I was blindfolded and led to an automobile; we drove around for about half an hour. Finally we parked. I was led down a flight of stairs and into a room and told to sit down and wait. In another half an hour I was led into a different room. My blindfold was removed and I saw a group of hooded figures in black robes gathered around an altar. Under the hood of the largest of these figures—directly behind the altar—I recognized the face of Bert. He began reading from a well-worn book a litany of oath and prayer and ritual in Latin and English. Now I noticed that there were about eight of us kneeling before the altar. One of them was Weintraub.

One by one we repeated the Latin mumbo-jumbo that would transform us into "brothers." One by one we vowed fealty and honor. One by one we were congratulated and sent back to the dorm for an hour's sleep before dawn.

It was much later that we found out what had happened: Weintraub *had* been blackballed because he was a Jew. Our threat to resign had bitterly divided the fraternity into two groups. One side wanted to blackball me and half a dozen others who were outspokenly sympathetic to Weintraub. The other faction wanted all of us to be initiated. It was they who held the reins of power. On their own, they went ahead and initiated us while their less charitable brethren slept.

The fraternity became my anchor, the source of the only stability I could find in a university that seemed to be making a determined effort to strip away every middle-class notion that had heretofore formed my idea of the world.

It monopolized my extracurricular time; I ate lunch and dinner there every day. On weekends I would go there for parties or outings to football games. I made few friends outside its harbor and cultivated the St. A "look" so that I could carry its reassurances with me at all times.

Of course, Weintraub would turn out to be the one brother I could not abide, who kept me awake night after night strumming his out-of-tune guitar. (I was convinced he did so just to torment me.) He disliked me too—challenging my authority almost every Monday night when I presided over meetings in the chapter room; trying to date whatever girl I happened to be liking at the moment; even, on one occasion, losing his temper and swinging at me over a room assignment I had made. I would come to dislike him as much as anyone I had ever known—and he, me—perhaps because it was easier to despise me than to feel grateful to me for getting him into the fraternity in the first place. And yet our enmity would contribute to the best lesson I would take with me from Columbia: that God might well be dead, but Fate, at least, was alive and had a sense of irony.

Charles Van Doren taught a course, my freshman year, in eighteenth-century English literature—the metaphysical poets, mostly. Skip Johnson, a brother at the Hall who had appointed himself my academic mentor, asked me if I'd like to sit in on one of Van Doren's classes. Indeed I would. Van Doren's name had been appearing almost daily in newspaper stories. He had testified before a New York County grand jury that he had not been given any answers to the quiz program questions. But as Van Doren maneuvered to evade a subpoena from a congressional subcommittee investigating the growing scandal, it appeared increasingly likely that the engaging, curly-headed professor had committed perjury. I very much looked forward to getting a look at him and was even interested in what he had to say about eighteenth-century English literature. As it turned out, the only thing I got to hear Van Doren say about the metaphysical poets was that "John Donne would never have gone on 'Twenty One.'" After posing briefly at the rostrum for a *Life* magazine photographer, Van Doren said that would be all. The photographer then marched the rest of us out onto the steps of Low Library for a class picture. I felt guilty passing myself off as a regular member of the class. But Skip said don't worry about it and I thought what the hell, how often do I get a chance to get my picture in *Life* magazine?

The article never appeared. Events had passed it by. By the time Van Doren's next scheduled class came around, he had admitted lying to the grand jury. Moving with a speed rarely seen in academia, the university had accepted Van Doren's resignation within twenty-four hours of his admission. Skip said that a young instructor named Jeffrey Hart was going to fill in for him. Would I like to come? Sure, I said; after all, I didn't want Skip to think my curiosity was limited to figures in the public press.

For that day the class had been assigned several poems written by John Donne. Jeffrey Hart led us slowly through one of the best known of them, "The Good Morrow." It came as a surprise to me to discover that it was about a man waking up from a night of lovemaking with his mistress. I hadn't expected seventeenth-century clerics to muse about "sucking on country pleasures" or describe lying nude in bed with a woman, "My face in thine eye, thine in mine." I was even more intrigued to learn that the poem was politically motivated. Hart explained that mid-seventeenth-century England was swirling with revolutionary currents. Donne found strength in coherence and constancy and felt threatened by the Reformation, by Francis Bacon's attacks on a priori reasoning, and especially by the political upheavals that would lead to the beheading of Charles I in 1653. To a man like Donne, these events foreshadowed the end of rationality and order. His poetry reveals an attempt to retreat, to reestablish an orderly world, even if its boundaries extend no further than the four walls of a bedroom:

> For love, all love of other sights controls,
> And makes one little room an everywhere.

> Let sea-discoverers to new worlds have gone;
> Let maps to other worlds on worlds have shown;
> Let us possess one world; each hath one, and is one.

Sitting there listening to Hart talk about John Donne, I realized how silly I'd been to begrudge Columbia for not being Williams or Princeton. I thought how little it mattered whether there were pep rallies or winning football teams. For the first time I felt part of the place.

"Please see me." Did I realize right away what those words meant? I don't know. It had been a humiliating autumn learning how little I really knew. There was some solace in discovering that Plato and Aristotle had pretty well resolved all those lonely questions I had wrestled with so vainly the year before. But that was small comfort, surrounded as I was by minds more impressive than my own. It was one thing to read them, another to find them all around me, even among my classmates: How were they able to locate allegory in the *Iliad,* or know what Aristophanes was satirizing in *The Frogs,* or spot Freudian overtones in Aeschylus? How did they make historical connections and catch allusions and two-thousand-year-old puns so quickly?

While my inability to keep pace with the reading list of Humanities A-1 somewhat undercut my high opinion of myself, my Contemporary Civilization course was wreaking even greater havoc on my self-esteem. "CC," as it was called, is the bedrock on which the Columbia education is built, a mandatory course that attempts to ground each student firmly in his Western cultural heritage by leading him through the seminal documents of its development. It was, and remains, a noble idea, but the speed at which the course moves has peculiar side effects on those who take it, rather like observing the world's great art through the window of a speeding automobile.

The effect that CC had on me—no doubt precisely the one desired by my professors—was to strip me of certainty about almost everything. For Monday, I might read Paul of Tarsus's assertion that "as Christ was raised from the dead by the glory of the Father, we too might walk in newness of life." For Wednesday, skip a thousand years to Moses Maimonides's insistence that Christ received "fitting punishment" for his sacrileges. For Friday, it might be Aristotle calling democracy a "perversion," or Cicero sounding vaguely Marxian. Simple pieties that I had held dear—the nobility of work, the benevolence of elected leaders, the evils of communism—became increasingly suspect as I was exposed, eloquently but disturbingly, to other possibilities. The harshest knowledge of all was learning that what we knew as truth was scarcely more than possibility, and that the only truth we could ever know for sure was that truth was impossible to know.

That perception came later. At the time I ascribed my distress and perplexity to a failure of either intelligence or will, I wasn't sure which. With guilt came fear: I had fooled Columbia into letting me in; it was only a matter of time until I would be found out. And *booted* out!

Unless—there was one chance for me. Was I not the winner of the Eustace S. Glascock award for creative writing? Had I not been exempted from Freshman Composition? Maybe I did confuse Aristotle with Cicero and wasn't sure any more what I believed about God and social systems and American foreign policy. Never mind about that, I could *write,* couldn't I? I was a *writer*. That would see me through.

"Please see me." That's all the paper had on it. No grade. No other comments. Just that. It was my first paper, an essay I had worked on four nights running for my Advanced English Composition class, the one class I had treated myself to in a schedule otherwise made up of required courses. My paper analyzed Dr. T. J. Eckleburg, the billboard oculist whose eyes brood over the Long Island landscape in *The Great Gatsby*.

I had read *Gatsby* diligently. Twice, in fact: the first time for pleasure, the second time with a particular eye for Dr. Eckleburg's symbolism. The trick was to figure out what he stood for. I decided Dr. Eckleburg was God.

He may well have been. But the problem was less with my judgment than with my expression of it, filled as my writing was with pretension, cant, and malapropism. At one point, I suppose in warning of the dangers of reading too much into Dr. Eckleburg, I wrote: "One devoted to the art of 'creative reading' can no doubt obtain magnanimous [sic] significance from the most simple expositions, even deriving, for example, some philosophical revelation from, say, Bugs Bunny." I also exhibited a flair for imagery: "Mr. Fitzgerald has woven the warp. Now he moves to braid the woof. The forecasted intertwining of these threads spells the tragic climax and completes the silken robe that is the novel."

When I went to see him at the appointed time, the professor, an effeminate man who combed his thinning hair forward to resemble a cheap toupee, appeared even more nervous than I. He took a quick puff of his cigarette and, with a jerky sweep of his hand, waved me to a seat.

"Ah, yes, Mr. Winfrey," he said after another quick puff. "You are a freshman, I believe."

I admitted that that was indeed the case.

He smiled. That gave him his out.

"Yes, I thought so. Your paper displayed a certain . . ." he took a deep drag on his cigarette as he searched for the proper word, *"unfamiliarity* with the style of the critical essay."

I told him that I didn't know quite what he meant.

"Yes," he said, "I can understand that. Perhaps if you were to take a look at some of Professor Trilling's essays, that might be useful. The one on Sherwood Anderson, for example, and of course the one on Fitzgerald. You'll find them both in *The Liberal Imagination.*"

I said I would do that.

"You also have a tendency to confuse . . ." he inhaled deeply, "convoluted sentences with good writing, and to . . ." he exhaled, "use a big word when a small one would be more appropriate. Because this is your first . . . *try,* I'm not going to count it too heavily."

I stood outside his office breathing deeply. Then I went to a bookstore and bought a paperback copy of *The Liberal Imagination.*

I worked even harder on my next paper, an analysis of the character of Gabriel Conroy in James Joyce's short story "The Dead." For nights on end, my assignments in other courses untouched, I flailed away at my typewriter. At last I was satisfied. I felt in command; there was a new maturity in the prose, a reasoned, balanced judgment. The professor had been right: the first paper *was* embarrassingly puerile.

The Gabriel Conroy paper was returned: "Please see me." I was crushed. I went to the professor's office the same afternoon.

"You wanted to see me, sir?"

"Oh, yes, Mr. . . . Winfrey." A puff from the cigarette. "I think you're making progress. Yes, progress. But you must relax a bit. You still have a tendency, I'm afraid, to use an erudite word merely because it is erudite. And that tends to give a sense of . . . of *strain* to your, uh, prose."

I nodded thoughtfully, though I felt near to tears.

"And you waste a great deal of space in writing out your mental processes. It is with the, uh, *results* of those processes that we are concerned. I'm giving you a C-plus for the paper."

"Yes, sir," I said. My God, I thought, for a C-plus I'm behind in all my other courses.

My next paper earned a B-minus and an encouraging notation: "A valiant effort at a stylistic analysis and a commendable try. Keep working in the direction suggested by this paper."

And on the next, miracle of miracles, a B and more encouragement: "Your writing is improving in smoothness and clarity."

And then another B: "You continue to improve both in clarity of organization and in the logic of argument."

I spent most of Christmas vacation working on a long paper about James Joyce's attitude toward women in *Portrait of the Artist as a Young Man*. The paper, on which our final grade would be largely determined, was the longest and most ambitious scholarly project I had ever attempted, perhaps forty pages in all. Turning it in, I felt confident. I felt even better getting it back with a B-plus emblazoned on the top. As I sat there feeling smug and satisfied, I scarcely heard the professor say that he would be leaving the course; something about scheduling difficulties having to do with Charles Van Doren's dismissal from the university. We would like the new man, he assured us.

I worked hard on the first paper for the new teacher. I felt I had learned a great deal about literature, about writing, about expressing myself clearly and concisely. I had also learned to use such words as "epiphany," "alienation," and "ideology" correctly, as well as phrases like "thematic unity" and "cultural assimilation." I was anxious to have my confidence affirmed by someone new and I was certain, as I handed in my deftly expressed insights about Joseph Conrad, that it would be. A week later the new professor handed back the paper. "Please see me." I dropped the course.

Just as demoralizing, in a different way, was my rejection by Van Am and Blue Key, the two service societies that each year selected a dozen or so freshmen from among the multitudes to work with the university administration and to be universally acclaimed for having been selected.

Interviews for this honor, each lasting about fifteen minutes per candidate, began one morning and lasted through the night. I was called about midnight for my first interview. My hands were sweating as I walked through the door and seated myself before a battery of weary upperclassmen. I stated my name, and a junior whom I recognized as having led the rally for Charles Van Doren asked me the first question.

"How would you define a jock?"

"A jock," I said. I paused a moment, reflectively. "I would say a jock is an athlete."

The junior feigned indignation. "I'm a varsity tennis player," he barked. "Are you calling me a jock?"

"Well," I said, "on one level, yes. What you're suggesting is that 'jock' also has a pejorative connotation. And of course you're right; in some contexts it does suggest anti-intellectualism. I wouldn't say a tennis player would necessarily be considered a 'jock' in the second sense."

The junior looked disgusted with my answer.

Someone else asked me what I expected to get out of Columbia. I gave a rather unoriginal response about gaining an understanding of what was known and what was not known about man and his place in the universe.

Someone interrupted my answer to say that on Van Am one was expected to distribute a lot of circulars and that this activity required a good, strong voice.

"How loud can you yell?" he asked.

I screamed at the top of my voice.

There were a few more questions. Did I remember the dialogue between Marlon Brando and Rod Steiger in the scene in the back seat of a car in *On the Waterfront*?

"Something about 'I coulda been a champ. I coulda been somebody,' " I said.

They said they'd let me know.

The Blue Key interview went pretty much the same way.

Three days later the preliminary lists came out. I had survived the first cut for Van Am but had been eliminated from Blue Key. I took it hard.

My second Van Am interview was scheduled for 3:00 A.M. a few days later. I set the alarm for two and went to sleep. I woke up at ten minutes to three. The alarm hadn't gone off. I jumped from the bed, threw on a suit and tie, and raced downstairs to the interview room. The committee had just about given up waiting for me when I arrived.

I breezed through the questions. I took it as a good sign that I had awakened in time. I felt relaxed and confident. When it was over, I went to my room and slept soundly and happily. Two days later the list was published. My name was not on it.

I sought out one of the upperclassmen who I felt had been particularly sympathetic to me during the interviews.

"Well," he said, "I tried for you. But I couldn't convince a couple of the guys. It was your smile. All during that second interview you kept smiling. They said it was unnatural."

Later I heard that I had been beaten out by a guy who, when asked a question he thought particularly inane, told them he wasn't about to answer such a stupid question, said they could stick Van Am up their ass, got up, and walked out. I wished I had had the balls to do that. It took me quite a while to get over not getting into Blue Key and Van Am.

In time, in other courses, I learned to write the kind of papers the Columbia English Department deemed acceptable and was able to churn out B-pluses with relative ease. If I rarely got an A, I ascribed it more to my sloppiness (I found proofreading too painful) than to any lack of "seriousness." Seriousness or, as we preferred to call it, "moral seriousness," was the highest calling. Frivolity—or worse, commercialism—was the gravest failing.

I was serious about myself and the *experience* of college rather than about the actual work I was supposed to be doing there. It was so much easier to talk about literature and literary criticism, about John Crowe Ransom and Allen Tate and the New Critics, about Stanley Edgar Hyman, I. A. Richards, Sidney Hook, F. R. Leavis, and Lionel Trilling (*always* Lionel Trilling), than it was to sit in a library or a dormitory room or a fraternity house reading and reading. It was so much easier to go off to the West End Bar or to gather in somebody's room to talk about literature or girls or the Bay of Pigs or fallout shelters or the Berlin crisis.

We did not talk all that much about politics. Nor did we have much to say about the causes that would so occupy the thousands who would follow us into college in the mid-1960s. We talked *ideas:* skepticism and paradox and ambiguity, cultural assimilation and isolation, the purpose of literature and of life, angst and eros and thanatos. When we spoke of Culture, and we often did, it was understood that we spelled it with a capital "C" and did not mean things like opera and drama or good books. We meant Life.

There was very little that we didn't know something about: from baseball to Berlioz we could usually come up with a sentence or two that implied a greater knowledge than we actually had, and greater skepticism than we actually felt. We had formed few of our opinions ourselves. Rather, we had absorbed what we thought from our teachers, each other, and the air. We knew, or thought we did, that Hemingway was over the hill, that Mailer and Bellow and Roth were comers, that Wyeth was commercial but Pollack a genius, that Fellini prostituted himself and Antonioni didn't. We knew that television was trash, that the best movies had all been made, that Broadway was for tourists, and that *Time* magazine was not to be trusted.

We were, without knowing it, elitists. We devoted the better part of our waking hours to studying the meaning of life without ever stopping to wonder by what stroke of good fortune we had been granted the time and freedom to do so.

My mother took a job my freshman year as the "social hostess" on an old German liner converted to Caribbean cruise duty under the American flag. I joined her on the ship for a three-day cruise to Nassau at spring vacation. She had wangled the first mate's cabin for me at no cost, taking advantage of the mate's vacation and the grizzled old German captain's crush on her. I was to sail to Nassau and wait there while my mother and the ship shuttled to Miami and back. I'd join the ship again on its next leg back to Miami.

I met Millie the first night out in a lounge near the ship's bow. I was eighteen. She was twenty-five, a Cleveland schoolteacher who had graduated from a college I'd never heard of called Kent State, best known, she explained, for its wrestling team. I told her I was a Columbia senior. I got a bottle of champagne left over from the welcome-aboard reception and we went out on the bow for some fresh air. It was chilly outside and we huddled together to keep warm.

She stayed with me in the first mate's cabin that night. In the morning I scrounged up two glasses of orange juice while she slept, then tripped coming into the stateroom, spilling it all over myself and feeling like a fool. She said I was a funny fellow.

Later that morning, in a handicraft store off Bay Street, watching her delight the native saleswoman with her warmth and friendliness, I fell in love with her voice—softer than any I had ever heard—and then with her laugh, which was as easy and natural as a Nassau breeze.

While she continued to shop, I slipped next door and bought a jade ring for her.

When we got back to the ship, native boys were diving for coins off the third deck. I told Millie that I would dive off the fourth deck, one higher than the native boys, just to show her how much I cared for her. She laughed. She thought I was kidding right up to the moment I dived off, a slow swan seventy-five feet to the water's surface. Although I wasn't hurt the current was strong. I had to swim several hundred yards around the stern of the ship to a ladder on the dock. I was nearly exhausted when I pulled myself out.

The look on Millie's face when I came off the ladder made the stunt seem worthwhile. She looked anxious and relieved all at once. She said I was crazy and I said, "Yes, about you."

That night we joined a group from the ship for a tour of Nassau nightclubs. At one of them I took out the ring I had bought and slipped it on Millie's finger. Millie took my hand and kissed my little finger. Then she kissed me softly on the lips.

We swam the next day and lay together in the sun. In the late afternoon we said we'd write to each other. Then we said good-by. I stood on the beach and watched as the ship steamed out of the harbor, realizing at just that moment that I'd made a terrible mistake. I had met the girl of my dreams, had wooed her and won her, and now I was letting her sail out of my life. I didn't know what to do. I went to a bar and had some drinks. I felt miserable. I left the bar and returned to my hotel for a restless night's sleep.

On the beach the next day I met a pretty, dark-haired divorcee from New York City. Maybe I could forget about Millie, I thought. The divorcee agreed to have dinner with me. As the afternoon wore on, I thought more and more about Millie. Finally I told the divorcee that I might not be able to take her to dinner after all, that I was thinking of flying back to Miami instead.

"Oh," she said, "I was so looking forward to it."

"You were?" I said. It occurred to me that there were possibilities I hadn't considered. Perhaps I could get Millie out of my mind yet. I started talking very fast.

"Listen," I said, "I've never said anything like this to anyone before, but, well, this is a special circumstance and . . . if I stayed, would you, that is . . . well, do you think we might go to bed?"

The divorcee did not slap my face as I half-expected her to. She smiled. She said well, she'd never had it put to her quite so matter-of-factly before but that—though she wasn't promising anything—she thought the possibility far from remote.

I thought to myself that things like this didn't happen to me. To others, perhaps, but not to me. Then I realized that, even so, it wasn't going to be enough. I wanted to stay; I wanted to wake up next to this very attractive woman. But I thought about Millie. She would be flying back to Cleveland in just two more days. I wanted so much to see her again before she went back to a routine that I was not a part of. I wanted to somehow seal what I knew we felt for each other.

"Listen," I said to the divorcee, "I've really had a good time today and I really like you. I'd love to stay and go out with you. But I can't. I just can't. It's too complicated to explain, but it has nothing to do with you and I hope you understand." Then I threw my things in a bag, took a taxi to the airport, and got on a plane to Miami.

My mother was furious. She had found out that I had let Millie stay with me in the first mate's cabin. She had found out about my dive off the side of the ship. She had even discovered a receipt for the jade ring and had, as she put it, "put two and two together." But most of all she was furious because I was supposed to be in Nassau waiting for her and the ship to return, and here I was instead in Miami. I felt terrible. I apologized to my mother. "I'm sorry," I said, "but I think I'm in love."

Of course I had no idea how to find Millie. I didn't know where she was staying. I just had to count on running into her. I figured that she would probably spend the day shopping on Lincoln Road, so I walked up and down Lincoln Road, certain that she was near. I spent all day and most of the evening walking back and forth, watching heavily made-up matrons displaying their jewels and mink coats in the seventy-degree weather. But I didn't find Millie.

The next morning I somehow remembered which airline Millie had flown down on. As I knew she had reservations back the next day, I called the airline. A reservations clerk said she was sorry but she was forbidden to give out any passenger information. I put down the telephone and thought about that. Then I called the airline again. A different young woman answered. I told her that I had found a pocketbook containing an airline ticket made out to a Miss Millicent Turner. I didn't know how to get in touch with Miss Turner. If they could please contact her and give her my name and telephone number, Miss Turner could then call me and I could return the purse to her. The girl sounded skeptical but she agreed to do as I suggested. I sat by the phone to wait. Twenty minutes later it rang.

"Hello, lap dog," she said. "What's this about a purse and what are you doing here?"

"I came to see you," I said. "The purse was a ruse."

She laughed.

I picked her up at seven and took her to the most expensive nightclub in the most expensive hotel in Miami Beach. A young singer named Bobby Darin sang his hit recording "Mack the Knife." I held Millie's hand under the table and for the first time in days felt happy.

After the show Millie turned serious. "I found out, you know," she said.

"Found out what?" I asked.

"Your age. You're only eighteen. I'm twenty-five."

"What difference does that make?" I asked.

Millie said, oh, it was so complicated. She said that just last year she had fallen for one of her students. He was only seventeen. She was still seeing him. The difference in their ages made things very difficult. Part of the reason she had come to Miami was to forget about him, maybe meet somebody new. Instead she had met me. She was afraid she had some terrible weakness for younger men.

I said it didn't matter how old she was or how many men she had known before me or how young they were. What mattered, I said, was us.

She kissed me and said I was sweet. We'd see, she said.

The next day I drove her all around Miami, showing her places where I had grown up. In the afternoon I took her to the airport and put her on a plane for Cleveland.

When I got back to Columbia, I called her to say how much I missed her. Almost every night I wrote her a long, single-spaced typewritten stream-of-consciousness letter, full of zest for living and my longing to be with her. I wrote about everything I did, everything I thought and dreamed, and told her how very much I loved her.

She came to New York for a weekend and I hitchhiked to Cleveland for two more. I met her friends. And, on an excursion to her hometown, I watched Lawrence Welk on television with her mother and father in their paneled basement. I wondered if I'd ever be a part of this warm and loving family. I would sometimes talk of marriage but she would say, "Sssshhh."

Over the years I've given so many different reasons why I joined the Marines that I'm no longer sure just why I actually did. I used to tell people that I had been deceived by the "universal" in that Eisenhower phrase "universal military training" and had actually believed that everybody got drafted sooner or later. Since I had to go anyway, the logic then proceeded, I might as well try to get something out of it. I would further explain that McDonogh had taught me the advantages of being an officer. And the Marines had the best program for becoming one. That part was true enough. The Marines' platoon leaders' course was scheduled, sensibly, in two six-week summer increments. That was better than devoting four years—giving up what amounted to a full year of college—to courses in tactics or naval history or leadership. Then too, I used to talk a lot about "challenge."

Eventually I came up with another explanation. "Ever since I was a little boy," I would say, "I always wanted to be an *ex*-Marine." I always hit the "ex" with a kind of verbal wink to insure that the listener got the joke.

And finally, if I were feeling philosophical, I might borrow one of my professor's insights into a Wordsworth poem that every son must kill his father in order to become like him. Perhaps that one came closest to the truth after all. Perhaps I had to prove to my father, as well as to myself, that I could take whatever it was the Marines were going to dish out in order to be free to be myself.

Whatever the reason, I signed up for the platoon leaders' course a couple of weeks after the start of my freshman year. My orders to report to Quantico the following June arrived just after Christmas.

I spent a good many afternoons that spring running in Riverside Park and doing chinups and pushups.

I reported, nervous but eager to have the shock of whatever was in store behind me, to Penn Station one bright June morning for the special train to Quantico. I spent the ride trying to gauge my fellow candidates, listening to an ex-enlisted man who had been through Parris Island tell us it was "gonna be some rough shit, man."

As the train slowed, I looked out the window to see a dozen stone figures staring in at us, their hands on their hips, their jaws thrust forward, their faces all but concealed by Smoky the Bear hats: DIs—drill instructors. Waiting in line to get off the train, I heard shouting and the sound of running. By the time I reached the platform the scene was chaos: DIs yelling while my fellow PLCs scampered and stumbled, trying to get into the long ranks that were forming parallel to the train.

I joined the confusion, dropping my duffel bag and freezing to attention in rank in front of a red-faced hulk who seemed to have been chiseled out of some leftover boulder from Mt. Rushmore. What I saw of his face was an open mouth: "Move! Move! Move!" it said. I stood stock-still, hoping to become invisible. The man on my left was less fortunate. Getting into the rank, he stepped on the sergeant's shoe.

The sergeant grabbed the unfortunate fellow by his madras shirt, lifting him to his tiptoes.

"You fahking step on my fahking shoe," he bellowed into a frozen face an inch from his nose. "You fahking step on my fahking shoe. You fahking step on my fahking shoe," the sergeant repeated to the form in the now-torn madras shirt.

Then a man on my right did something that filled me with admiration and terror: he laughed. The DI's nose flared and his eyes blazed with incredulity. He let go of the madras shirt. Slowly, he turned his disbelieving face past mine to focus at last on the man on my right. Out of the corner of my eye I saw my compatriot's smile curdle, his eyes fill with fear.

"You loffed," the sergeant said in a whisper. "You fahking loffed," he repeated in an accent I now perceived to be Scandinavian.

"Why you loff?" he whispered. "What so fonny?"

"Uh, uh, no, sir . . . I mean . . ."

"You fahking maggot." The sergeant's mouth was an inch from the man's ear. "You want to loff? Loff. I want to hear you loff."

Suddenly it got very quiet. Even the other DIs stared at the man on my right.

"Uh, heh, heh," the man on my right said tentatively.

"That is no loff," screamed the sergeant.

"Ha, ha, ha, ha, ha," bellowed the man on my right, his eyes filled with terror.

We were herded into large trucks, or "cattle cars" as they were called. Inside we filed onto four benches, paired to face each other. When we sat down our knees touched.

The sergeant screamed that if he caught just one of us so much as move a fahking muscle, he would ream our asses. We sat stock-still, straight and silent as tombstones, the forty minutes and twenty miles to Camp Upshur, a Quonset-hut city that would be our home for the next six weeks. It was only when we got off the buses that we realized our rigid silence had gone unobserved; the great Swede had stayed behind.

We were a platoon now. Gunnery Sergeant Broadacre, who looked to me like Eddie Arcaro, took charge of us: "Okay, you pukes," he said in a gravelly voice, "your asses are mine now." There was an unmistakable mischievous twinkle in his eye. We liked him immediately.

Marched to one of a hundred identical Quonset huts, we were assigned bunks and bunkmates. "Gunny" Broadacre told us we'd soon be able to eat off the gray cement floor, we would scrub it that clean.

We were marched to a huge gymnasium, where we filled out forms, forms, and more forms.

We were marched to the dispensary where, clad in socks and underwear, we were given physical examinations. ("Lower your shorts. Bend over. Take your cheeks in your hand. Smile.") The highlight of the medical exam came as we stood in line for our urinalysis, each of us holding a bottle containing a "specimen." A bored, weary Navy Corpsman handed each man a wooden stick, chemically treated to change color in reaction to sugar. To each of us—though by the time we reached him we'd heard his instruction forty times—he droned the same directions: "Take the paper off the stick, put the stick in the piss. Pour the piss in the sink, shit-can the stick."

We were marched to a warehouse and issued foot lockers, four sets of "utilities" (Marine fatigues), two pairs of boots, one pair of dress shoes, two sets of "tropicals," two sets of khakis, a complete inventory of "782 gear" (packs and canteens, pouches, and shelter halves), and a miscellany of notebooks, pencils, laundry bags, and shoe polish.

We were marched to the base barbershop, where we formed a line. It moved quickly. An Ivy League smoothie from Dartmouth, a hood from Detroit, a hayseed from Minnesota, and a jock from Kansas waited their turns at one end of the Quonset hut. Emerging from the other end were anonymous men with shaved heads. They were not marines yet, but they were no longer identifiable as any of the stereotypes that make for quick and easy assumptions about people.

We were marched to the armory and issued M-1 rifles. I was disappointed when Gunny Broadacre pointed first to his rifle and then to his fly, saying "This is my rifle and this is my gun. This one's for fighting and this one's for fun." I had already seen that routine in the movie *Take the High Ground,* with Richard Widmark, and I suspected that Gunny Broadacre had too.

While we waited in line—there were lines for everything—Gunny Broadacre began teaching us some drill.

"Der are two kinds of commands," said the Gunny in an accent I came to know as Marine Corps-ese. "First, you have your prepatory command: 'Ri-aightttt. Leffffff. Uh-bowwwwt.' Den comes da command of execution: 'Face!' . . . Got dat?"

Some of the candidates had trouble distinguishing their right from their left. If the Gunny commanded "Right, face" and someone turned left, the Gunny would say, "Your *other* right, stupid!" Habitual offenders extracted more imaginative insults from the Gunny's verbal arsenal. "You'd fuck up a Chinese fire drill," the Gunny might say. Or "You couldn't pour piss out of a boot if it had the directions written on the heel." Or "Are there any more at home like you?"

Gunny taught us to "Sound off!" and the first few times we yelled "One, two, three, four," the Gunny screamed, "My grandmother makes more noise than that!" Some of us suspected he wasn't much exaggerating.

It was well after midnight when the Gunny finally had us gather around a bunk to observe the correct way to make it up. Then he had us lace our new boots up, fill them with hot water, and put them under our bunks. Nobody asked why.

I fell asleep immediately. It seemed only a second later that I was awakened by what sounded like an enemy attack.

Lights were shining in my eyes. I didn't know where I was. In the center of the Quonset hut stood a man I had never seen before. He was big and ugly. He held a length of lead pipe in his hand and was beating it as hard and as fast as he could against the inside rim of a galvanized garbage can.

"Get up, get up," he yelled. "Get your fucking asses up. Get up, get up!" All around me people were scrambling out of their beds. They looked confused, standing on the floor in their underwear, uncertain what to do first.

Suddenly the big man with the pipe stopped beating the inside of the garbage can. He came fast down the row of beds, clanging each with the pipe, metal on metal. When he saw a human form under blankets he'd lunge at it, his hands pushing the mattress from underneath and sending it and the body it supported crashing to the floor.

That was our introducton to Platoon Sergeant Drake, the assistant DI. He had a big beer belly, fingernails bitten to the cuticle, and mean eyes.

We dressed, pouring the water out of our boots, putting them on wet and squishy. We lined up in the darkness outside the Quonset hut. My watch read ten minutes past four. We double-timed to a black-topped, football-field-sized parade ground known as the "grinder." We double-timed four times around it, chanting "One, two, three, four—we love the Marine Corps" and "Hop, hoo, Cindy Lou." We double-timed to the mess hall to find ourselves at the end of a line an eighth of a mile long. Forty-five minutes later we entered the mess hall. Like a broken record Sergeant Drake told each of us: "Take all you want. Eat all you take."

We were given twelve minutes to eat and get outside in formation. We were marched back to our Quonset hut for an inspection of our beds and lockers. We were introduced to our platoon commander, Lieutenant Lakely. He had a jaunty look about him. He bounced on the balls of his feet when he walked. Scuttlebutt had it that his father was a Marine general. That might account for his cockiness. I was just thinking that when he asked the platoon at large who could type. That was when I made my mistake. I raised my hand. He wrote down my name. He'd see me later, he said.

At the end of a day filled with hour-long classes in the M-1 rifle, the field-marching pack, and the chain of command, a couple of hours on the grinder learning "close-order drill," another hour of calisthenics—including perhaps a hundred pushups in expiation of various infractions committed either individually or as a platoon ("You've done it again, people; you've pissed me off!")—Sergeant Drake called out my name.

"Shitbird," he said, "report to the platoon commander's office on the double."

"Sir. Yes, sir," I yelled in the prescribed manner—at the top of my lungs—and raced to the Quonset hut that was reputed to contain the platoon commander and his office. As instructed, I stood outside the door, banging the frame with my fist three times as hard as I could. Finally from inside came a voice, bored and disgusted.

"I can't hear you."

Again, harder still, I banged three times. I could feel my fist swelling with pain.

"Yeah. What is it?"

"Sir. Candidate Winfrey reporting as ordered, sir!"

"Get in here."

I opened the door and stepped forward into the darkness. I saw the outline of a desk and made for it. Unfortunately, I chose a diagonal rather than square route.

"You asshole," said Lieutenant Lakely. "Get back outside."

I went outside and waited. Nothing happened. I banged the door frame again, three times, with my swollen fist.

"I can't hear you," came the voice from inside.

When finally I had properly presented myself to the platoon commander, I was shown to a desk and a typewriter.

Lieutenant Lakely handed me the results of the morning's

physical tests. I was told to read off the name and score of each man while he entered them into a notebook.

Every time I read off a particularly low score, the lieutenant would shake his head and mutter "Great, just great" or "Swell." Near the end of the list I came upon the lowest score of all. Anticipating the lieutenant's disappointment, I said something to the effect that Candidate So-and-so hadn't put in such a stellar performance.

"Candidate!" The lieutenant turned on me, his eyes wide with anger. "Nobody asked you for any smart-ass comments. The Marine Corps doesn't need any smart asses." When he calmed down he confided, "You and I are not going to get along."

He turned out to be right. Throughout the six weeks he rarely passed up an opportunity to single me out for special censure. When he found out from my four-page "autobiography" that I had gone to military school, he took to shaking his head at me, saying "prior military experience" with feigned disbelief.

I got onto Sergeant Drake's "shit list" too. It was easy. I got a high score on the Government Classification Test, a sort of military IQ exam. Sergeant Drake had a theory about intelligence. There were two kinds. There was GCT intelligence and there was common sense. They were mutually exclusive. Sergeant Drake based his theory on the fact that he had scored poorly on the GCT. Knowing himself to be a repository of common sense, he naturally concluded that my high score on the GCT was irrefutable evidence that I, as he put it, was "one dumb shit."

"Candidate," Sergeant Drake never tired of reminding me, "you may think you're smart because you got a high GCT, but let me tell you, you are *one dumb shit*. Aren't you?"

"Sir. No, sir!"

"You callin' me a liar?"

"Sir. No, sir!"

"Well, then you must be."

"Sir, the platoon sergeant is invariably right in military matters but the platoon sergeant is incorrect in assuming that the candidate is a dumb . . ."

"The platoon sergeant is invariably," he mimicked in a high voice. "Oh, fuck, Winfrey. You're so fuckin' dumb . . ." His voice would trail off as he walked away in disgust.

Actually, I didn't much mind my little exchanges with Sergeant Drake. They helped break the monotony of interminable, tedious days. And, as it was a game he seemed to enjoy, who was I to interfere with my platoon sergeant's pleasures?

Our days were spent on the go, from five in the morning until ten at night: running, doing pushups, sweating in hot classrooms, drilling, running the obstacle course, getting chewed out, standing for inspections. Some days, after a morning of classes, drill, calisthenics, more classes, and more drill, I'd look at my watch with disbelieving eyes. Instead of indicating late afternoon, as it should have, my watch would insist it was only ten o'clock in the morning. At that rate, it would take days to reach nightfall. I would force myself to stay awake after taps to savor the silence before it all began again an instant later.

Toward the end of the first week we took our first forced march. It was only a three-miler, but the sun was high and we carried heavy packs and rifles up steep hills and through mud up to our knees. Our platoon brought up the rear of a company spread out over nearly half a mile, which meant that no matter how slow the pace of the company commander, we would always be running to catch up. He had the longest legs of anyone I'd ever seen. Sometimes, running to catch up, we'd come huffing and puffing to the crest of a hill and spot him, two hills ahead of us, running.

About two miles out a tall, quiet boy from Minneapolis veered out of line, fell to the ground, and clutched his stomach. A sergeant came up to him, felt his forehead, and concluded that he was faking.

"Get your slimy ass up, you maggot," the drill instructor yelled.

The man moaned and opened his eyes. He struggled to his feet and rejoined the long rank. But a few hundred yards down the ravine, as we ran back through the muddy swamp, he dropped out again, clutching his stomach and moaning. The sergeant called for a truck to take "the pussy" away.

By the time the rest of us returned to the barracks an hour later, the boy from Minneapolis had almost finished packing. In another hour he was gone, the first to wash out. "Da United States Marine Corps," said Gunny Broadacre, "does not tolerate malingering." Then he added that people who are seriously ill on hikes do not grab their stomachs or moan.

The hikes were terrible. Each week they loomed ever more frightening as their distance and our load increased. When we had at last finished a hike and dragged ourselves back to wash caked red clay off our clothes and equipment, I'd feel euphoric. I remember taking a shower after the first hike, rapturous as the hot water poured over my beaten body, feeling that it was too much pleasure all at once, that it was *too* good, that I didn't deserve it.

Each week too, the sun got hotter, and the pace faster. On the second one, a seven-miler, I made a lasting friend about four miles out when, in an act of incalculable mutual generosity, we each spit a mouthful of precious canteen water on the other's neck.

The third hike almost did me in. We had scarcely left the base, with fourteen miles in front of us, when I felt my underwear crawl up to chafe my already raw inner buttocks and thighs. Then, about an hour and a half out, the long rawhide lace on my right boot came undone. There was nothing I could do about it. In an attempt to minimize the killing "accordion effect," Gunny Broadacre had ordered us—under peril of extinction—to hold on at all times to the entrenching tool hanging from the pack of the man in front of us. I was, therefore, a link in a chain; I couldn't pull out.

Each time the right foot of the man behind me hit the ground, stepping on the dangling lace, my stride was broken. It felt as if someone was jerking on a rope around my ankle as I ran. For more than an hour I stumbled and limped along until finally, near exhaustion and ready to give up, I pulled myself out of the line (ignoring the obscenities) and bent over to tie my bootlace in the underbrush.

I had only half-tied it when I heard the sound of someone crashing through the bushes behind me. I caught only the barest glimpse of Sergeant Drake before his boot lifted me in the air and sent me sprawling.

"What the fuck you think you're doing?" he yelled at the prostrate figure on the ground in front of him.

I pulled myself up on my elbows and glared at him. "Sir," I said through teeth clenched in a rage I was fighting to control, "I . . . was . . . trying . . . to tie . . . my fucking . . . bootlace."

"Why you little shitbird," Sergeant Drake yelled. "How dare you swear at me! I'm gonna have your ass." He headed toward me, fists clenched. I took off, propelled by fear and adrenalin, my bootlace still untied.

Those of the weary troops plodding along the dusty trail who chanced to look off to their right saw two figures sprinting through the woods, bobbing like jack rabbits, a great hulk of a man in heated pursuit of a much smaller one. One of those who did see us was a lieutenant from another platoon. He tackled me.

"Thanks, lieutenant," Sergeant Drake said through great inhalations of breath. "The little pisser told me to 'fuck off.' "

"Sir. No, sir," I said, gasping. "That's not what happened."

"I don't give a shit what you say happened," the lieutenant said. "Get back in line. We'll take care of you when we get back."

I never did get my bootlace tied.

Back at the base I didn't even have a chance for a shower before I was summoned to see Lieutenant Lakely, who had missed the hike because of "administrative duties." He had already heard Sergeant Drake's version of events. I told him mine.

"Winfrey," said the platoon commander. "What you did out there today could have cost lives in combat. You could be court-martialed for what you did. I've told you before, you're too goddam much of a wise-ass. You've got two strikes against you. One more and that's it, you're out."

It's funny how dire the threat seemed at the time and how terribly cowed I was by it. "You're out." What "out" really meant was that instead of having to spend three years on active duty as a lieutenant, I'd be sent home to join a reserve unit as a private. I would then fulfill my military obligation virtually as a civilian, giving up only one weekend a month and two weeks for summer camp. The platoon leaders' program was, in fact, a draft dodger's dream. But at Camp Upshur, in the summer of 1960, "You're out" meant ultimate disgrace. It meant failure. It meant that you were cut from inferior goods. The third of us who either gave up or were washed out became objects of derision and pity.

Just as they had been at McDonogh a decade before, my days organized themselves around mail call, a daily ritual at which the Gunny carried his usual vulgarity to even greater heights. No letter ever passed from his hands without some comment geared to humiliate the recipient and entertain the rest of us. If it looked to be perfumed, the letter was invariably detoured by way of the Gunny's large nose. "Oh Jesus, dis one gives me a hard on," he might say. Or "hey, dis smells familiar. Yeah, dis is da chick a sailor friend a mine's been gettin' inta.'' It didn't matter if the letter happened to be from somebody's wife; the Gunny did not discriminate.

I came in for my share of what passed in the Gunny's case for wit. Particularly about halfway through when Millie's letters stopped.

"Hey, Winfrey, I tink she's found herself a civilian to fuck," was the way the Gunny put it when three days went by with no letter from her. I laughed along with everybody else. But when two more days passed with no word from her, I got anxious. When another two went by I was frantic. Finally I could stand it no longer. I stood in line over an hour to use the single pay telephone that candidates were allowed to use.

When I finally got through to her, Millie seemed surprised that I was so upset. She said she was sorry she hadn't written. No, there was no special reason, she just hadn't had anything particular to say. She said she'd write to me right away.

But nearly another week passed—five more devastating letterless mail calls (even the Gunny stopped making cracks)—before I heard from her again. Somehow I never felt the same about her after that.

After the second week we were given liberty from Saturday noon to late Sunday afternoon. Just before noon taxis from Washington began pulling onto the grinder. They would deliver any five of us to the Ambassador Hotel, an hour north, for a mere twenty-five dollars. It seemed a most wonderful bargain.

I was struck on the first of those rides by the world's remarkable resemblance to the landscape I remembered. It simply had not occurred to me that it would have gone on unchanged and seemingly indifferent to a universe bounded on four sides by screaming sergeants.

We checked into the Ambassador, where rumor had it that marines had been holing up on D.C. liberties since the French and Indian war. We were exhausted. The night before, none of us had slept more than a couple of hours—and that on the floor—in preparation for a "junk on the bunk" inspection (so called because every item of issue gear, from underwear to our M-1 rifles, had been laid out on our bunks in precise conformity to a photograph in the Marine Corps manual). Most of us, therefore, went right to bed.

I slept all afternoon, then made my way to the lobby, where I immediately heard a commotion coming from the bar. I looked in and saw Gunny Broadacre, surrounded by a dozen members of my platoon. He was obviously drunk, telling war stories about marching out of the Chosin Reservoir—the "Frozen Chosin"—in Korea in 1950 at Christmastime. My fellow candidates sat in rapt admiration, laughing with him when he said something funny, buying him another drink when he ran low. When I returned from a steak dinner two hours later, some of the audience had changed, but the Gunny was still regaling an admiring circle. He was there when I went to bed at midnight, and he was there the next morning when a bunch of us went out for pancakes.

He was very drunk when I came down for lunch at two (after sleeping most of the morning), and he was practically comatose when we piled into taxicabs for the ride back to Quantico at five. There was no sign of him by the time we hit the rack at ten, and somebody said that Sergeant Drake had gone to town to get him. I wondered what was going to happen when he didn't show up for a seventeen-mile hike the next day.

When the reveille lights came on at four the next morning, we were all a bit incredulous—and suddenly, strangely proud—to see Gunny Broadacre standing immaculate in perfectly starched utilities and spit-shined boots in the center of the hut, yelling at us to get our liberty-softened, pogey-baited, candy asses out of bed. During the hike, keeping a proprietary eye on the Gunny helped take our minds off our individual agonies. The only sign that he was hurting came from his utilities, which were drenched in sweat. That was the one hike that nobody dropped out of. I guess we were all thinking that if that little hungover sonofabitch can make it on two or three hours' sleep, then, by God, so can we.

It was right before the fifth one that I got a letter from my father asking me to remember that "no Winfrey ever dropped out of a hike yet." I came pretty close that day to becoming the first. It was a twenty-miler, mostly over the grueling firebreak trail, a fifty-yard-wide swath cut through Virginia's hilly pine forest as a protection against fires. The humidity was high and the July sun was especially hot. After three hours I saw no possibility of finishing. I was done in. I had run out of breath and sweat. I began to pick out a spot—twenty or thirty yards ahead—where I was going to fall. But when I reached the spot I took another step, then another, and another. Then I picked another spot to fall. In just that way I managed to finish the hike on my feet, miles further than I ever thought I could go. I felt proud. But the important thing I took away with me was a new understanding of what the body could take if it didn't have the brain to coddle it.

At the end of the hike we bivouacked for the night. We were ravenously hungry. We built a big bonfire and cooked our usually vile 1945-vintage C-rations. But no food ever tasted so good. I thought of Epicurus, the man most often associated with fine food and lavish feasts: "I am ever amazed," he is supposed to have said, "at the pleasure one can take from eating a piece of bread and drinking a glass of water."

There were many other lessons to be learned that summer, even at our "platoon party," for which we had rented a small ballroom at the Ambassador. We had festooned it with crepe paper and had bought bushels of pretzels and cases of beer. We had everything but girls. Nobody knew any girls in Washington.

Gunny Broadacre said he wanted "three volunteers: you, you, and you." I was the third "you."

"Okay, lover boys," he said, "get your asses out on the

street and round up some pussy. I don't care how you do it, I don't wanna hear any shitty excuses. Just do it. Remember," he said with an exaggerated wink, "only one out of three girls in Washington is a touch typist. All the rest are huntin' peckers."

I had never picked up a girl on the street in my life. I had never even had nerve enough to try. But the prospect of failing Gunny Broadacre was worse than saying "Excuse me, miss, but we're having a terrific party over at the Ambassador Hotel and . . ." Within forty minutes I had put a dozen different young women—nurses, secretaries, a librarian, two coeds, a legislative assistant—into taxicabs headed for the Ambassador.

We all got drunk that night, even Lieutenant Lakely. He got so drunk he told me that even though I was a wise-ass I wasn't such a bad marine at that. I even told him he wasn't so bad either. Only Sergeant Drake didn't make it to the party. He was in the hospital. He had suffered a heart attack on the last hike.

At "graduation" the next week we paraded in front of a grandstand full of colonels, generals, girlfriends, and parents. The day was dark. We thought for sure that it would rain. Then, just as the band began to play the Marine Corps Hymn—signifying our ordination as marines—the sun (I swear it's true) broke through the clouds, flooding the parade ground with warm light. Damned if my chest didn't swell and I didn't feel tears welling in my eyes. Just one more thing I hadn't thought myself capable of that summer.

VI

I returned to Columbia for my sophomore year to find a campus apathetic about the 1960 presidential election. Signs on New York City trash cans were carrying the slogan "Cast Your Vote Here for a Cleaner New York" and a lot of students and faculty seemed to think that would be a good place for political ballots as well.

I was suspicious of both candidates. Richard Nixon seemed darkly menacing. John Kennedy was too young, too glamorous, and too opportunistic.

And then came the first debate. As I'd been locked away at Quantico during his nomination in Los Angeles, it was the first real look at Kennedy I was able to take. Ten minutes into the debate I was won over. By the time it ended, I was a fervid New Frontiersman.

As I got deeper into my second year, I came to realize that Columbia's real "lions" were not the members of her various, mostly laughable, athletic teams. The real "lions" were the faculty. The ones I got to know best occupied a warren of offices on the fourth floor of Hamilton Hall, the main classroom building for undergraduates.

Columbia's English Department was as fine as any in the country, staffed as it was with such men as Charles Everett, Andrew Chiape, Richard Chase, F. W. Dupee, Quentin Anderson, Eric Bentley, and of course, Lionel Trilling. But it was two of the younger, lesser known men who would have the greatest influence on me: Jeffrey Hart, whose course in eighteenth-century English literature I was now taking, and Steven Marcus who taught the English literature of the nineteenth century. There could scarcely have been greater intellectual opposites.

Hart was a man of the century he taught. His hero was Edmund Burke, and like Burke, Dr. Johnson, and Jonathan Swift, he was devoted to stability and to those two things that historically best enforce it, institutions and religion. "One cannot reject a consensus of tradition," he would say, paraphrasing Burke approvingly. "Man has a contract with those who are dead and those who are yet to be born."

His philosophy aside, he was an excellent teacher, particularly on the poets, explaining, for example, why a good minor poet like Robert Herrick was of a different order from a major-leaguer like John Donne. (When a student protested his dismissal of Herrick, Hart said that a good minor poet was a fine thing to be. When the student challenged him by insisting that Herrick was major, Hart shrugged. "Maybe," he said. Then, as if an afterthought: "But if so he's the only major poet who never wrote a major poem.")

He was often able to come up with a new way to help us get a fix on things, like having us read a bad poem like John Dryden's "Upon the Death of Lord Hastings" so we'd appreciate the good stuff when we came across it.

> Was there no milder way but the Small Pox,
> The very Filth'ness of *Pandora's* Box?
> So many Spots, like *naeves,* our *Venus* soil?
> One Jewel set off with so many a Foil?
> Blisters with pride swell'd; which th'row's flesh did sprout
> Like Rose-buds, stuck i' th' Lily-skin about.

> Each little Pimple had a Tear in it,
> To wail the fault its rising did commit.

He often said he would like to edit an anthology of the best poets' worst poems; such a book would make it so much easier to appreciate the good stuff. The remarkable thing about that was that you could disagree with him thoroughly and yet listen to him with delight. In fact, disagreeing with him was an intellectual adventure that often led to the discovery of one's own beliefs.

He had married a pretty girl who knew next to nothing about literature. I liked him for that. She had gone back to college to learn about it, and I liked *her* for that. He had pixie eyes and a horsy laugh, and I thought it more than a damn shame when Hart was denied tenure, the ultimate academic affront.

He had written an article for the college alumni magazine in which he said that people who were uncertain of their place in the social hierarchy—the senator who never went to college, say, or the clerk whose ancestors arrived on the *Mayflower*—were apt to feel what he called *ressentiment*. Therefore, he argued, societies that encourage social mobility—universities, for example—were "anger factories."

To reduce such anger at Columbia, Hart's article offered three measures. "No doubt they will be found highly controversial," he wrote in what turned out to be understatement.

First, he proposed giving preferential treatment to sons of alumni in admissions and scholarships. Second, he urged the encouragement, even subsidization, of fraternities and clubs. Third, he said that courses in "the history of Christian culture" should be made mandatory.

The article caused a furor: he was the victim, I suppose, of bad timing. Just as most of the college community was beginning to awake to the plight of the black man, along came Hart saying that as "opportunities open up for Negroes we may expect their *ressentiment* to increase." As for social protest, he wrote that "surely one of our principal concerns should be to seek measures to discourage it, to moderate it."

Long before the article appeared in print—it had no doubt been leaked—rumors about it crisscrossed the campus. Hart began getting anonymous phone calls in which the word *fascist* was a common refrain.

One of the calls was not anonymous. It was from Lionel Trilling, who asked if it would be convenient to have lunch with Hart the following day at the men's faculty club. Hart said yes, of course.

"Well, Jeff," said Trilling after a few polite niceties had been exchanged. "We hear you have written quite an article."

"As a matter of fact, I brought it with me," said Hart, reaching into his breast pocket for the manuscript.

Trilling began to read. At last he finished. "Well now," he said, "that doesn't seem so bad to me."

Hart was about to thank him when Trilling began again.

"Now Jeff," he said. "You wouldn't ever consider writing for a magazine like William F. Buckley's *National Review* now would you?" Hart thought about that for a moment. Then he said that he certainly wouldn't rule it out.

No one who was not present at the deciding faculty meeting knows for certain why Hart was not given tenure. But it was widely assumed that it was the article, combined with his unfashionable politics, that did him in.

I didn't know much about his politics and didn't even understand the article. It was enough for me that he was a good teacher; no university ever has enough of those. Eventually he went to Dartmouth where he prospered.

Steven Marcus could scarcely have had a more delectable set of credentials. As a student more than a decade before, he had been one of Lionel Trilling's most gifted protégés. (A probably apocryphal Trilling seminar in which Marcus, Norman Podhoretz, and Allen Ginsberg spurred each other to ever more brilliant insights had become ingrained in Columbia lore.) He had won his field's most prestigious fellowship, a Kellott, to study at Cambridge under no less awesome a figure than F. R. Leavis, from whose prodigious head Trilling himself was sometimes rumored to have emerged full blown. Marcus had spent two years listening to Leavis, that fearsome autocrat, denounce false gods and decree the true: Jane Austen, George Eliot, Henry James, Joseph Conrad, and D. H. Lawrence, whom Leavis took due credit for immortalizing.

Marcus returned to Columbia in the early fifties to collaborate with Trilling in the abridging of Ernest Jones's three-volume biography of Sigmund Freud. In time, Marcus gained fame for his study of nineteenth-century British pornography, *The Other Victorians,* a book that did much to legitimize that subject as a fit one for academic inquiry. But in the days when I first knew him, he was making his reputation with articles about Freud and Dickens in *Commentary, The New Statesman,* and of course *Partisan Review.*

Even though his respect for Trilling found expression in an unfortunate adoption of the great man's mannerisms, gestures, even his inflections, Marcus himself was a riveting classroom maestro. Small in stature, he was nonetheless formidable. He dressed impeccably in dark tweeds, but sported a barbershop-quartet mustache that lent a rakish air to his otherwise stern demeanor. He was fastidious, both in his person and in his devotion to the study and importance of literature. His convictions—that a culture is defined by its literature and that esthetic judgments are moral judgments—were no less sincere for having been first propounded by his mentor.

Jeffrey Hart had made John Donne real and exciting to me, but Marcus ushered Wordsworth into the room as a guest. To hear Marcus read Wordsworth's "Old Cumberland Beggar" in a soft voice full of reverence was to hear poetry for the first time:

> Him from childhood have I known; and then
> He was so old, he seems not older now;
> He travels on, a solitary Man,
> So helpless in appearance, that for him
> The sauntering Horseman throws not with a slack
> And careless hand his alms upon the ground,
> But stops—that he may safely lodge the coin
> Within the old Man's hat; or quits him so,
> But still, when he had given his horse the rein,
> Watches the aged Beggar with a look
> Sidelong, and half-reverted . . .

"Mr. Winfrey," he whispered. For a second, I thought he was still reading the poem.

"Tell us, Mr. Winfrey, why the horseman stops, reins his horse, and puts the coin into the beggar's hand."

"Sir?"

"The horseman. What does the horseman feel when he sees the beggar?"

"Sir, I'd say he thinks . . . there, uh . . . there but for the grace of God go I."

Marcus's eyes shone.

I leaned forward expectantly.

"There . . . go . . . I," he said.

"Yes, sir."

Wordsworth, Marcus went on to say, was not the "nature poet" that so many people thought. He was fiercely interested in beggars, prostitutes, society's riff-raff—people on the periphery—because, as Marcus put it, "it is there, in the *extremities* of the human condition, that the essence of life exists in pure form. The beggar, for example, is as little alive as it is possible to be. And yet he *is* alive and, more important, has a function. People respond to him, the instinctive, unconscious response of one human to another. Therefore he humanizes, humanizes even the poorest of the poor by giving them a feeling of power—the power to help *him!*"

My favorite poem, from the first time I heard Marcus read it aloud, was "Tintern Abbey." Wordsworth wrote it when he was twenty-eight years old. He had returned to a favorite childhood spot a few miles above an old abbey on the river Wye. It was his first return to the country after five years of city living in London:

> Five years have past; five summers with the length
> Of five long winters! and again I hear
> These waters, rolling from their mountain-springs
> With a soft inland murmur. Once again
> Do I behold these steep and lofty cliffs,
> That on a wild secluded scene impress
> Thoughts of more deep seclusion; and connect
> The landscape with the quiet of the sky.

I swooned over the rhythm of the phrases. I could picture those waters rolling from their mountain springs. I could hear their soft inland murmur. Marcus told us that the poem was about mortality and recompense. Wordsworth was saying that although life is lived most intensely in youth, its loss in maturity is replaced by something even more satisfying.

> For I have learned
> To look on nature, not as in the hour
> Of thoughtless youth; but hearing oftentimes
> The still, sad music of humanity,
> Nor harsh nor grating, though of ample power
> To chasten and subdue. And I have felt
> A presence that disturbs me with the joy
> Of elevated thoughts; a sense sublime
> Of something far more deeply interfused,
> Whose dwelling is the light of setting suns,
> And the round ocean and the living air,
> And the blue sky, and in the mind of man:
> A motion and a spirit that impels
> All thinking things, all objects of all thought
> And rolls through all things.

"The still, sad music of humanity." How ardently did we listen for it. How certain we were that Wordsworth had indeed transmitted to us those "elevated thoughts" he had described. It was an exciting thing to be twenty and believe you were discovering the meaning of life.

In Marcus's class we sat around a large seminar table. By chance—or perhaps design—the table accommodated one student fewer than had been accepted for the course. The inevitable result was that one of us, the last to come to class, was left to take a chair to the side of the table, on Marcus's left. Invariably that chair would be occupied by Charles Wiseman, the most pompous young stuffed shirt I had ever encountered. Wiseman's haughty manner was accentuated by the fact that he seemed incapable of turning his head without also turning his body—whether from physical disability or from willfulness I never learned.

By the time Marcus arrived, professionally tardy, most of us would already be seated around the table. His entrance never varied. He'd walk into the class, put his books on the table, open the windows, brush the dust from his hands, sit at the table, open the book containing the day's reading, and pose a question—always the same one: "Well, what can we *say* about" whoever or whatever had been assigned for that particular class.

One morning Marcus had just completed his classroom scenario and was about to speak when Wiseman walked into the classroom and took the chair to Marcus's left. With great deliberation he began to remove his books from his cloth book bag. Marcus pretended to ignore him.

"Well, what can we *say* . . . about Carlyle's *Sartor Resartus?*" he at last asked.

The room was silent. Still fishing in his book bag, not condescending even to look up to be recognized, Wiseman mumbled that he "found it illegible."

"What's that? Mr. Wiseman?" Marcus's question was a whisper.

"I said," said Wiseman, perturbed at having to repeat himself, "that I thought it illegible."

"I believe you mean 'unintelligible,' " said Marcus without a hint of a smile, "unless, of course, you read it in manuscript."

Not many days later Wiseman returned to the fray.

Our subject that morning was *Pride and Prejudice*.

"Well," Marcus began as usual, "what can we *say* . . . about Jane Austen?"

Wiseman, his timing perfect, had entered the room at the moment the question was posed.

"I think she's a masochist," he said in a voice dripping with condescension.

"What's that, Mr. Wiseman?" Marcus's eyes shone.

"I said, I think she's a masochist."

Marcus looked as if he were not going to respond. He turned his attention to the book on his desk. Quickly he turned his head back toward Wiseman.

"Well, think again, Mr. Wiseman," he said.

And then there was Trilling himself.

Occasionally we'd spot him loping back or forth between his apartment on Claremont Avenue and Hamilton Hall, where he taught most of his classes. Sallow, he had perpetually blackened eyes. We were certain it was from all they had seen.

I was once surprised to discover him standing—like other mortals—in the takeout line at a local coffee shop, a vision no less jarring than if I had found President Kennedy hawking copies of the Columbia newspaper at Broadway and 116th Street. Another time I came across him in the Columbia bookstore. He was buying a fountain pen, trying it out by scribbling on a note pad on the counter. I waited until he had paid for it and left before going to the pad and ripping the top sheet off. Another startling disappointment: he had simply written his name again and again.

No one else on campus came close to Trilling as an object of speculation and gossip. Everyone seemed to know the story of the time he and Jacques Barzun got into a punning match. It began with a student quoting Malthus's "Honi soit qui mal y pense." Barzun qualified the student's remark: "Honi soit qui Malthus pense." At that, Trilling turned to Barzun, grimacing. "Honi soit qui mal he puns," he replied.

Another oft-told tale recounted the time Trilling was interviewed on television by David Susskind. Susskind began by asking Trilling if he'd read a certain article in that morning's *New York Times*.

"I'm sorry," Trilling is supposed to have interrupted him, "but I don't read newspapers."

In addition to the stories about him, we knew his habits. We knew that he spent his mornings writing in his study, then lunched, usually at the men's faculty club. His afternoons were spent teaching or reading. He had read, it was said, "everything there is to read in English"—meaning all the major novels by all the major novelists.

I had to wait a year to get into his course on the modern novel: Thomas Mann, James Joyce, D. H. Lawrence, and Ernest Hemingway.

Strangely, he wasn't the best teacher, possibly because he preferred writing, possibly because he had given the courses for too many years. But what we came to see, what commanded our awe, was his authority, his daring, whether it was in choosing to pronounce "rationale" to rhyme with "passion daily" or to pronounce *Our Mutual Friend* "unquestionably Dickens's best novel." He possessed a self-confidence so secure that it was at times indistinguishable from arrogance.

Once a student had the poor taste to suggest that a passage in Thomas Mann reminded him of the opening lines of *The Stranger*. Trilling shot a look that should have warned the young man he was out of line. Trilling began searching for another raised hand.

The student persisted, as if he thought Trilling had simply not heard him. "You know, *The Stranger*," the student said.

There hung in the air the unfortunate suggestion that perhaps the novel was unfamiliar to Trilling.

Trilling fixed the student with a black-eyed stare. His voice was barely audible as he asked, "Do you mean the novel? Or the play? Or perhaps it was the short story you had in mind?"

Still unaware that he was being played for a fool, the student said, "The novel. You know, that's the one where the guy gets the telegram that says his mother just died."

"Oh, that one," whispered Trilling with consummate disdain, calling on another student.

Another student—in a graduate course I audited—answered Trilling's question about a Wordsworth image with the word "amoeba."

"I beg your pardon," said Trilling, his eyes narrow.

"The image—spreading out—like an amoeba. You know, the one-celled animal."

"Mr. Robinson," said Trilling. The condescension was edible. "Wordsworth didn't know from amoebas."

Another time Trilling asked the class at large where the novel assigned for that day's class was set.

A student raised his hand and was recognized. "The modern consciousness," he answered.

"Yes," Trilling nodded, "but I'm looking for something a little more concrete." He called on another student.

"The postwar world. Disillusionment," said the second student.

A pained expression appeared on Trilling's face. "Actually the answer I was looking for was *London*," he said.

Sadonna Sawyer was so beautiful she made me feel miserable the first time I ever looked at her. She was blonde and willowy. She was also my friend and fraternity brother's date. Jack had told us about this goddess he had met at Vassar, but the Christmas party at the Hall was our first opportunity to meet her. He hadn't overstated her charms. She was quiet and stood apart that night from the general mood of forced revelry. I liked that.

She came to the Hall a lot after that on weekends, staying just down the corridor in Jack's room. Sometimes I would hear her voice coming through my door and I would feel as lonely as I had ever felt.

Then in the spring she stopped coming. Jack told me he was going to Europe that summer with a girl from Sarah Lawrence.

"But what about Sadonna?" I aked him.

"What about her?"

"Well, what's *she* doing this summer?"

"I don't know," he said. "I think she said something about coming to New York."

Funny coincidence: I was going to be spending the summer in New York also. Having nothing better to do, I had enrolled in Columbia's summer program.

Jack went off to Europe. I started going to summer classes. Taking a chance one night I called the Vassar Club and asked for Sadonna. When she came to the phone, I nervously asked her if she would like to go to a movie on Friday night.

After the movie we walked through the streets of New York and talked late into the night. The next day I called her and asked if she would like to have dinner with me that night. I was very happy to hear her say yes she would. After a week of dinners and movies she came to live in *my* room at the Hall. I had never lived with a woman before and it both delighted and frightened me.

From a Journal—June 1961:

Sadonna constantly on my mind. State of elation after dry, brittle year. First emotion for a woman since Millie. Relationship complete and complex but not entangled yet. We have loved and sworn on it but neither of us is sure.

(And of course there is Jack; I may be on the rebound.) But she is with me now and it looks promising and perhaps even wonderful.

Compelling urge to write after long abstinence. Probably from stimulation of reading *Ulysses*. I'm enthralled by its complexity; makes me feel alive to life, as if waking from a sleep. Life seems at once terribly exciting, complex, and sad. Joyce almost makes words seem sufficient. One of my old bugaboos is that the great emotions cannot come across through words alone. Now I'm not so sure.

Got involved in a long discussion today about communism. I defended USA. Admitted many faults with America but came to the conclusion that I am willing to die for her. If not for the America I know, at least for the ideals of America, the heritage and responsibility placed upon me by her history. I'm not a free soul. I'm just learning to question my existence and see relevance in it. God, there's so much to learn. And, I'm told, so many ideals to be shattered. How I hope not.

July 12:

My mind is preoccupied with who Horatio Alger is. Who is Logan Pearsall Smith? Who is E. B. White? Reading Kafka's *The Trial*. Plan to study this weekend. Resolved: to use the library more, to write more, to work more, to sublimate and abstain more (for both our sakes). Delighted with my crewcut. Delightful to be less vain, more outgoing, less morose—all thanks to Sadonna. She's many people in one—most of them I like. But my big worry is: Am I good for her; am I corrupting her? Perhaps I'm not as "liberal" as I like to think. Perhaps I'm not strong enough to break with convention, even though I'm convinced it is mostly bunk—except as it is effective for the masses. Is that pragmatism? Roy Villa would know—he's so damn positive about things. But he made a mistake in encouraging me to read William James. Now Villa sounds like warmed-over James.

What is the *Crossroads of Liberalism?* Is the liberal stand sturdy? No, unless reinforced by tradition. See Jeff Hart. Ask who wrote that essay on English society and the one about Russell Kirk and Jacques Barzun. Who is Russell Kirk?

Have learned so much sexual technique. I look at people and smile inwardly because of the wonderful secret Sadonna and I share. (Can't say I've done much to keep it a secret; must learn more discretion.) Today is one month after Sadonna's and my first date. She's the greatest experience of my life so far. What about the future? How long will I maintain this journal? Long enough to record our marriage (at least five years away) or to record other girls (at least one year away I should think)? Oh, the uncertainty of it all.

Letter from Peter set me to wondering about the Marine Corps. It's a test I've got to pass, but is it the best thing for me? What about graduate school?

Exhilarated by writing class. Mine the best paper. Everyone liked it. Teacher said "rare insight." Have to rework it though. Comments were mainly favorable. Criticism justified: poor ending, illogical. Jesus, life is exciting sometimes. Now to read.

Professor Dodson:

Large, brooding eyes surrounded by puffy flesh and topped with an overly generous amount of curly hair which entwines and reentwines in itself and seems to be held in place only by this entwining. Small chin, scarred cheeks, small mouth with pouting, protruding lower lip which is stretched in smiling. His smile is more of a reply to a dentist's request for him to show his teeth—clenched. About 5'9". Baggy wash-and-wear suits with orange calfskin, crepe ripple-soled shoes. Walk so soundless. Voice is oratorical, precise, vocabulary intense. Marked repetition of favorite words: archetypal, propiatory, scatological. An actor thrives under his academic heavy skin. Large hands, sweaty, puffy, but not fat. Long arms, probably from heavy work long since terminated. Heavy neck, Adam's apple obscured by sagging, liquid skin. Aware, yet at times tortured expression of a man who has seen the light and feels impelled to show others. In short—tired, inconsistent, lecturer of at times brilliant insight.

July 13:

Things to find out about: T. S. Eliot's "objective correlative." Also, the relationship of the Huxley boys—Thomas, Julian, Aldous. Idea for a theme—the effect of "The Little Engine That Could" on the psyche of children.

Ran in the park about a mile. Pooped. Worked on rhythm; kept mouth closed. Perhaps I ought to keep it closed in other endeavors as well.

Psychology exciting for the first time. Talked in subjective terms about Freud, Jung, Adler. (The pragmatic approach is valid in some instances but incomplete.) Interesting that psychology is so philosophical. In the psychologist's attempt to make his field empirical, he throws out a lot of useful information and still does not approach any sense of objectivity.

July 14:

Russell Kirk is president of C. W. Post College and may be the most profound conservative thinker. C. P. Snow revels in technology. W. F. Buckley is editor of *National Review* and writes good prose. Walter Lippmann is usually considered conservative. Grayson Kirk and A. W. Griswald are "gutless." The Turner Report traces American ideals and institutions to the frontier experience. All this from Dave Loomin.

Today I saw a woman pull up in a Rolls Royce to buy bread at Gristedes. I saw a club-footed photographer in a red Corvette. Saw a young Columbia janitor dressed like the hip hood he probably is, a poor man's Fabian or Sal Mineo. I bet he's big with the girls: long hair, thick lips, big white teeth, pointed shoes, conceited looking, and wearing a heavy sweater in ninety-degree heat over a chartreuse shirt and narrow pants.

July 18:

Saul Bellow spoke today. My question is: When the nun in the audience told Saul Bellow that she thought he was the expression (in fiction) of his hope for fiction (in the lecture) and added that she bet he had never had a nun for a fan, was she expressing some sort of repressed individualism or speaking for nuns everywhere?

When Bellow was asked if he thought writing could be taught in the classroom, he answered, "Can sex be taught in the classroom?" Everybody laughed, but I'm not so sure.

Afterward I asked him about the ending in *Seize the Day*. He asked me what I thought and I said the scene in the mortuary was a kind of epiphany that would bring about an existential realization for Tommy. Bellow smiled and said that was what he was trying to do, and I swooned. He has kind eyes, a wonderful, almost sly grin, and a masculine slovenliness that is most becoming.

Bellow's view of the novel is to satisfy the need for some relevance to the chaos he sees about him. He says that modern novels are too didactic. Mann says the same thing. Art requires form. Mann's insight into the plurality of the artist seems valid. But he denies the plural existence for the true artist in *Tonio Kröger*. I suppose I'm seeking the in-between. I want to be that lieutenant who reads his poetry. Why is this less valid than the bohemian? Kerouac offers nothing except idealized self, which is relevant to no one but himself.

July 19:

Midnight reflections: reading Mann makes me wonder about my future and the Marine Corps. Really a tough decision. On the one hand, the obligation, the challenge, my father. On the other, the wasted time, the postponement of graduate school, three years in an anti-intellectual atmosphere. What is to be done with my life? Mann says if you're going to be an artist, be one, but it's a curse. Am still torn by the conflict between body and mind, environmental and objective ideals.

It had been the best summer of my life. When Sadonna went back to Vassar in September, we would talk to each other every night on the phone. On the weekends, she would come to New York to be with me or, less often, I would go to Vassar. That was how I got to actually meet Lionel Trilling.

He had been invited to Vassar to speak to a standing-room-only audience in the school chapel; it was, I thought, a brilliant reworking of one of his favorite themes: the relationship of anarchy to culture.

After the speech, when we had all repaired to a lounge for the three C's of Vassar social life—cookies, coffee, and conversation—an extraordinary thing happened. Sadonna and I stood at the outskirts of a ring of people—the entire Vassar English faculty—surrounding the great man. They seemed threatening to converge upon him, perhaps to squeeze the meaning of life out of him, when suddenly he broke through the ring and headed directly for me, his hand extended.

"So nice to see you," he said with an enthusiasm I had never observed in the classroom. He began pumping my hand. "Are you here?" he asked.

Am I here? Am I here? My mind raced. What in the hell does he mean, am I . . . ? Then I figured it out. He must have recognized me from class and think I'm a former student now teaching here.

"Uh, no, sir," I finally managed to say. "No, I'm still at Columbia, a, uh, *student* at Columbia. Just came up to see a friend"—I nodded vaguely toward Sadonna—"and to . . . heh, heh . . . hear you speak."

For a second he looked at me uncomprehendingly. Then he nodded.

"Well, nice to see you. Nice to see you," he said as the circle re-formed to engulf him.

I spotted him at once the next afternoon on the platform at the Poughkeepsie train station as he made his way to the train for New York City. I let him get on first, debating with myself whether to sit with him. Finally, taking the events of the past evening as a sign, I got on the train and walked to his seat. I asked if I could join him.

"Certainly," he said.

He was cordial but cool. Gradually, as I poured out my admiration for him, he warmed to me. I was very familiar with his work. I told him that even before I knew I was coming to Columbia my high school English teacher had told me about a speech Trilling had made on the occasion of Robert Frost's eighty-fifth birthday. Had he really called Frost a terrifying poet?

"All I said was that I didn't think Frost was the homey, cheerful, and fortifying poet that most people make him out to be. I meant terrifying in the sense of awesome or imposing. It was the press," he said, "that turned the whole thing into a cause célèbre. I had never much cared for Frost, thinking him a rather sentimental celebrator of American rural life. But on rereading him I discovered quite a different Frost, a Frost whose roots were much more in Greek tragedy than in *anything* American. In a way I was trying to rescue Frost from his admirers. Of course the press made much of the fact that I had compared him to the bald eagle. The point was that Frost, like the eagle, is a national symbol. And every child knows that the bald eagle is not bald at all but is distinguished in maturity by its shock of white hair."

I told him that I had enjoyed his speech of the night before. He said he was very grateful that I had been there, particularly afterward when my familiar face gave him an excuse to break away from "all those dreadful people." He shook his head in dismay and confided that he did not hold the Vassar English faculty in high esteem.

We talked about writing and writers and I told him of my ambitions in that direction. Trilling said that college was really a waste of time for a writer, that the best writers had simply *written,* and that the only training for a writer was doing it. He said that he had learned to write, he supposed, in the course of writing his book on Matthew Arnold. I said that however he had learned it, he had learned it well, and that I thought he had raised the essay to a level that it had not seen since Charles Lamb.

"Thank you," he said. "Indeed," he added, after considering the idea, "I'm not altogether certain that I haven't."

To my disappointment, I noticed that we were now passing through Harlem. I couldn't believe that the trip had gone so quickly. We shared a taxi to Columbia and I marveled at witnessing Lionel Trilling kibitz with a taxi driver about Mayor Wagner. I thanked him for the taxi ride and we shook hands. He said that it had been a most pleasant experience to meet me and that he had enjoyed "our little talk."

We never spoke to each other again, and though I continued to take his course he never gave the slightest acknowledgment of our having met. I would have been disappointed if he had.

It was not too long after the Trilling weekend that Sadonna and I drifted apart. It was my fault mostly, mine and circumstance. Sadonna had made me feel attractive for the first time in my life. I was eager to test my new confidence. And the enticements right in Columbia's own backyard proved beyond my meager powers of resistance.

One of my fraternity brothers, a graduate student in the Business School, had a brother who was unhappy at the University of North Carolina. He was thinking of transferring to Columbia. Would I meet him and talk with him, perhaps help him to make up his mind? I said sure.

I liked Porter Thorpe right away. He was unpretentious, and had a good sense of humor. Within an hour I felt I'd known him for years.

I told him he wouldn't be able to transfer to Columbia College, the small, liberal-arts division of the university; the college wanted all of its men for four years. But I said I was sure that General Studies, whose students included both adults and transfers from all over, would be happy to have him. I said I thought he'd like Columbia and added that I, for one, hoped he made the move.

He arrived on campus my junior year and took a small, windowless garret in an old building on the same street as the Hall. It was so typical of Porter, whose financial worth was in the uncounted, bonded millions, to live in so humble—no, so shabby—an apartment.

The more I got to know him the better I liked him. He liked me too; he laughed at my attempts at wit and listened to me as if I were some sort of junior sage. I think we found in each other what we feared was lacking in ourselves. To me, Porter represented an inherent sense of assurance; I liked the sense of understatement and modesty that found expression in his rattly old Volkswagen, frayed tweed jackets, and old cracked shoes. I suppose Porter took me for some sort of intellectual guide, someone to introduce him to the new world he was discovering at Columbia, someone to focus his new ambition to be a writer. Having switched his major from history to English, he needed all the help he could get. I knew the names of the players, not only Coleridge and Wordsworth and Thackeray but Trilling and Chiape, Anderson, Chase, and Dupee. More than that, I knew what they were about, what they stood for, how to deal with them. I had learned to talk a good academic game, cocksure and anecdotal. And Porter made the perfect audience. He believed.

The one thing that Porter had trouble believing was that Ann Allen had a crush on anyone, least of all me. He had known Ann from Boston long before she came to Barnard. He had also known most of the legions of boys who had fallen for her. What he had never known was anyone that Ann had fallen for or even that she ever could. For a while, after I first told him about meeting her—how she came right up and introduced herself to me one afternoon at the bookstore—he was skeptical.

I had to admit I was skeptical at first too, though I was rather proud of having risen to her announcement that we were going to be friends with what I thought was a pretty good rejoinder: "Okay, but in that case we ought to take off all our clothes and swim across the Hudson River together. Then, at least, we'd have something *real* to talk about—how cold or dirty it was, how tired we were, the view from New Jersey—something. We wouldn't be able to bullshit each other." She said that was the best idea she had ever heard.

She was easily the most daring girl who had ever expressed the slightest bit of interest in me. Even more amazing, her interest appeared to be far from slight. *She* would call *me!* She would suggest we have lunch together! Sadonna seemed far away.

Ann had won every boy she had ever set her eyes on. Her interest in me was directly proportional to my lack of interest in her, a lack I was feigning with ever-increasing difficulty.

Porter found me at the fraternity house one Sunday night about three weeks after Ann and I had first met. His eyes were wide.

"It's incredible," he said. "I gave Ann a lift down from Boston, and she talked about you constantly. I don't know what you're doing, but keep it up."

The next day she came to the Hall. She carried a package under her arm.

"These were my father's," she said, handing me two framed prints. "He had them on his wall at Harvard." She kissed me and left. I felt ecstatic. I wanted to sing. I wanted to go get Ann and take her away with me and live happily ever after with the most beautiful girl I had ever seen.

I called her that night. I said I wanted her to come with me to a party at the fraternity the next Saturday. She said she would.

On Thursday she called me. She was sorry, she said, but she couldn't come to the party after all. It had to do with an old friend of hers, a boy at Harvard. He was in some sort of trouble and she had to be with him. I said I understood.

I moped around all weekend. Finally, Sunday night, she called. She was back.

"I want to see you," I said. "I want to see you now."

She came to my room. I told her how much I had missed her. I told her I wanted to be with her all the time.

"No," she said. "I don't want that."

"Well, what do you want?"

"What I want is . . . a friend I can kiss."

I reached out and pulled her to me. I kissed her hard. She pulled away.

"I'm going now," she said.

I pleaded with her to stay but she shook her head.

I called her all the next day. Finally I reached her. I told her I had to see her. She said she'd meet me at the Gold Rail, a Broadway bar and restaurant where we had often eaten lunch together.

She looked more beautiful than I had ever seen her.

"Ann," I said. "I can't just be a friend you can kiss. I want more than that."

"You can't have it," she said. "You can't."

"But . . . but, I love you. Don't you understand? I *love* you."

"Don't say that. I don't want you to love me."

"I can't help it. I *do* love you."

Calmly she picked up a glass of water and threw it at me. I sat there, stunned and dripping, as she left the restaurant. I didn't try to stop her.

A few days later I met Lisa. She came to a party at the Hall, admitting afterward that she had been attracted more by curiosity about the fraternity than by the awkward young man who was her date that night. I was dateless as usual but, unusually, by choice. Through some deft maneuvering, I had inherited the fraternity bar, which I ran as a small, unlicensed business. Even charging only fifty cents a drink, I was able to make a tidy bit of pocket money—several hundred dollars a semester.

To her date's discomfiture, Lisa spent most of that night sitting by the bar. We talked.

The next day she agreed to come as *my* date to the next party. I found someone else to run the bar that night. By midnight we were making love in my room, hurriedly, because she had to take a 1:00 A.M. bus to Ithaca to see her boyfriend, Steve, a Ph.D. candidate in physics at Cornell. Since I hardly knew Lisa and still thought of Sadonna as my girl, I felt confused by the jealousy that came over me when Lisa left.

In the next few weeks I saw her as often as she would let me. When we were together, I felt certain I could win her away from Steve. I would come by the library, where she worked after school, to pick her up for dinner.

"Do you go out overnight?" I'd ask, as if she were a book.

"Mr. Winfrey!" she'd answer in mock indignation. Then she'd paraphrase the rule for reference books: "You can take me out overnight but I have to be back in the morning."

We'd have dinner at the fraternity or at one of the restaurants that comprise the gastronomical wasteland surrounding Columbia, then go to my room at the Hall to study or listen to music, read, and make love. After a few days of such a regimen, I could easily believe that I was the only one she cared for. We never mentioned Steve. Then the day would come when she would tell me that next weekend, or the one after, she would be going to Ithaca.

Those weekends were torture. She would promise to call me on Saturday or, if not, Sunday for sure. I'd wait around my room, morose and numb, for the phone to ring. Sometimes she *would* call; more often, though, she wouldn't get a chance. My imagination would then take over with scenes of its own masochistic devising. By Sunday night I would find myself at the bus station, nervously waiting for her to arrive. The Ithaca bus was invariably late. Just as invariably, my coming to meet her would turn out to be a mistake. She'd arrive tense and tired, unable to make so quick a transition from one pair of arms to another.

In the spring I changed my "official" Marine Corps address from the fraternity house to her parents' house in Cleveland. That way I was able to get the Marine Corps to pay my way from Cleveland to Quantico for my second summer of officers' candidate school. I went out to Cleveland right after exams.

I stayed with Lisa and her parents. Unknown to them, we also rented a tiny, shabby cottage at a lakeside motor court. We'd tell her parents we were going to the beach, returning hours later after a sunny afternoon without a hint of suntan on our bodies.

I wasn't much looking forward to going back to Quantico. I had heard that the second summer was tougher than the first, a thought that filled me with dread whenever I let myself dwell on it. (I was even less certain I wanted to spend three years in the Marines at all.) I guess the reason I finally made up my mind to go back the second summer was to find out just how bad it would be.

As it turned out, it wasn't all that bad, a result more than anything else of the luck of the draw: the new company commander had shorter legs than his predecessor; Sergeant Drake was nowhere to be seen; and Lieutenant Yarrow, our platoon commander, didn't feel in the least compelled to prove himself a hotshot. (He even had a sense of humor. When somebody asked him why he wasn't married he said he'd always been told that if the Marine Corps wanted you to have a wife they'd issue you one.)

We slept, that second time around, in brick barracks on the

main part of the Quantico base, a few yards from the railroad tracks of the Atlantic Coast Line. Each train—a dozen a night—sounded as if it was coming down the middle of the barracks. Invariably, the engineers leaned on their diesel horns a full half-mile before and after the Quantico crossing; the sound was like a buzz saw cutting through the skull. Those were the main differences between the two summers: the trains and Lieutenant Yarrow. We had hit it off so well that after the six weeks were over we began to correspond. My letters invariably focused on the question uppermost in my mind: whether or not to accept the commission that I had now earned.

August 15, 1962

Dear Bob,

    I found myself nodding almost continually in agreement as I read your letter. I know that I can get a lot out of the Marine Corps, and the way to do it, as you say, is to take the good qualities of those about you and make them your own, to learn from those you don't respect, find out why you don't respect them, and make sure that you have none of their adverse traits. The thing that really frightens me is that I'll stagnate intellectually. I don't mean that I'm any overpowering intellectual—far from it. And that's the trouble; for me to use my mind at all, I have to be around people who use theirs and force me to use mine to keep up. I know that there are plenty of intelligent people in the service, but intelligence is no good unless it is applied. Applying intelligence toward wiping out the maximum number of "gooks" in a given problem is wasting intelligence. It has to be used to solve the problem of why we're even fighting.

    A friend of mine was just released from the Army. He had been called up about a year ago for the Berlin business. "You know, if I had the strength of my convictions," he said to me, "I'd be a conscientious objector. But that would be just too difficult." I must admit to a certain sympathy with his viewpoint. I see the need for a military force. I see the need for a tough stand against Russia. I realize that appeasement is suicidal. And yet the absurdity of war, the horrors of it, are going to be that much more repelling when for the next three years I will wake to the fact that I am a professional soldier whose duty tomorrow may be to kill people—people who as individuals have no hatred for me and whom I as an individual have no hatred for. It's a frightening proposition, and getting killed myself is not nearly so frightening as is the thought of having to kill. I don't know what the answer is. Perhaps it would be best if the leaders of the warring nations fought each other alone, Kennedy vs. Khrushchev, or whatever. But I suppose the loser would get pissed off and the bombs would start anyway.

Columbia is an incredible place. There are some wonderful minds here and they don't give their students any answers, just the problems to be worked out for themselves. It's a wonderful and frightening and exciting place to live, and there are times when I think I'd be a fool to ever give up the academic atmosphere. Then at other times the material values of the world beckon and I think I should become a lawyer or even (ultimate prostitution) a business executive. I get anxious to get married and have children and then I say no, I mustn't, not yet. Ah, it's such a difficult but exciting time of life, to be twenty-one and unsure. My life must be so different from yours right now—really cushy. I have an apartment which I share and no real responsibilities and enough cash on hand that I don't have to worry. My girl will return in a few weeks and then I will just play for about six months, taking the fourteen points I need to graduate in February, and playing. And then in May I'll be at Basic School, asking myself what in hell I'm doing there, why I'm wearing a uniform and playing these ridiculous games of glorified cops and robbers, and what it all means.

VII

I moved out of the Hall and into my first apartment in the fall of my senior year, across the street from Grant's tomb, sharing it with a young bachelor banker I had met that summer. Lisa returned to Barnard in September; she stayed with me in the apartment three or four nights a week and those weekends she didn't go to Ithaca. By then I was hopelessly in love with her. And I was miserable.

Shortly before Christmas Steve came to New York for a weekend. Lisa promised, as she had been promising for more than a year, that it would soon be over between them. She also promised that she was no longer sleeping with him. I tried hard to believe that both things were true.

That Saturday night I stood watching as a Broadway audience filed out of the theater presenting *A Man for All Seasons*. Finally I spotted Lisa and Steve and trailed them as they walked, holding hands and laughing, to a restaurant. I waited outside, in the winter's cold, watching them through a window. An hour later, I followed them as Lisa led the way to one of "our" favorite places, an intimate little club where a quiet kind of jazz music complemented the wine and cheese.

I followed them in a taxicab to the apartment where Steve was staying. I stood outside and watched the lights go on in the apartment. I wanted to believe that Lisa would soon be coming out. I waited, hoping against reason. But the lights went off and no one came out. Finally I went home and moaned into my pillow until sleep came over me at last.

I can't remember a day that took longer to end than the next, a Sunday. By the time she called at last to say that Steve had gone back to Ithaca, I was practically out of my head. We had a terrible argument and I said I never wanted to see her again. I retracted my invitation to her to come to Florida for Christmas. I would use the time, I silently vowed, to wean myself from her.

From a Journal—December 24, 1962:

> The day before Christmas and all through the house, it is windy outside but sunny, and the clouds are racing along in front of the sun. This is my third day home, my third day alone with thoughts and memories and anxieties. I'm dreaming more than usual, many dreams, little scenes flashing along my unconsciousness. Mostly of Lisa, at least she's there somehow. It is difficult enough not to break down and call her now, these two weeks, with more than a thousand miles between us. What is going to happen when there are only three hundred yards between us?
>
> I must not see her. I must not. I cannot see her. She awaits like the surgeon's knife to emasculate me, to rob me of strength and dignity and self-respect.
>
> I will not let her. It is better to be lonely than to have her on her terms, her selfish, unnatural terms. I will not. I will be strong. Unless. Unless she gives up Steve.

January 7, 1963:

> Today is my second day back in New York City. Even after an absence of little more than two weeks I find it a

difficult adjustment. The city is gray, gray, and I'm in a very highly charged state of anxiety. I don't know exactly why. I haven't heard from Lisa since the twenty-first of December and refused to call her. However, she called me tonight and asked me to meet her for coffee. Reluctantly, I agreed, knowing that it would only depress me and complicate things. It was a rather awkward meeting. Unfortunately, she looked terribly beautiful, which only made me more nervous. Finally I got away without showing any of the terrible pains I feel for her—or maybe I did show them. I have the feeling she wants me back but only on her terms, and I will accept only complete and unconditional surrender. I must not weaken! I must not give in to her. If it means loneliness, if it means desolation, I must not give in to her. Too much is at stake; not only my self-respect, which is indeed something, but my whole future relationship with women. I cannot let the pattern that has developed repeat itself now or it will repeat itself for the rest of my life. I must suffer now to be stronger later. This is not too great a price to pay. I know that it is not. I will not give in.

Christ, I wish I were over her. Why did she have to come back? Why did she have to call? Why did she have to look so beautiful? And, most of all, why did she have to intimate that she wanted me? Why can't I be left alone? Why can't I just be satisfied with my loneliness? Why am I so weak? Why do I want her to call me right now, even knowing that if she did I would have to be strong and not invite her to go anywhere, not encourage her? Why, most of all, why, why can't she get over Steve? Why can't she love me as much as I do her? Why is all this so comically tragic, with me caught in the middle? Oh, please, if there is a God, please give me some kind of peace, some kind of half-contentment; even resignation will do. Please!

I called her the next day. "Can you come over right away?" I said.

The next few months were the best we ever had. Sometimes, on those nights when she couldn't stay with me at my apartment, I would come to her in the Barnard dormitory. It was a terrific risk. If I'd been caught, both of us would have been suspended from school.

I'd wait till after midnight, then make my way to a manhole at the corner of 116th Street and Broadway. Once the street was deserted, I'd lift the cover and slip into the bowels of Barnard, down through sewage pipes and heating ducts and storage rooms. I'd wind my way through this catacomb to emerge at last in Hewitt Hall. Next I'd walk past a sleeping guard at a desk, then up two flights of stairs and across the hall to Lisa's room.

One quick knock and I'd be inside, my heart beating so loudly I'd fear it would wake up the housemistress three rooms and six walls away.

We'd make exciting love those nights, inflamed by the danger of discovery. I'd sleep fitfully until, well before the first light, I'd dress and be off, reversing my steps to emerge a few minutes later into an eerie, still, fluorescently lit Broadway.

Porter spent a lot of time with us those days. He had no girl of his own and would come over to the apartment for lunch or dinner. Or he'd go with us to a movie or to the little Chinese restaurant that was always a special treat. He never seemed to mind going home alone when the evening ended and resisted all our attempts to fix him up with Lisa's friends.

The phone rang early one morning. It was my aunt calling to say that my grandfather had suffered a stroke and was in the hospital. My father would be flying in from California late that night. I should go stay with my grandmother in Queens.

My father arrived the next morning about dawn. We went almost immediately to the hospital.

I couldn't believe it was my grandfather. The toothless man in the bed looked nothing like him. The old man was out of his head, hallucinating about "spirits." He kept trying to get out of the bed; a metal railing held him in.

When my father saw my grandfather's vacant stare and his hollow cheeks, he broke down in tears. My father turned away from me, toward the window, and covered his face with his hands. I had never seen my father cry. It had never occurred to me that he could. I went toward him, I think to put my arms around him. I put my hand on his shoulder. Then I took it away. I thought I would cry too. And then I didn't.

My father regained his composure by launching an anxious inquiry into the kind of care my grandfather was getting. The doctor assured him that everything possible was being done.

That very night, after feeding him, an orderly left the railing off the bed. My grandfather tried to get out of bed. He fell onto the floor. He landed on his hip and broke it.

When my father heard about what had happened, he was livid. He stormed into the hospital and berated the doctor who was responsible. The doctor said he was sorry. He said my father could continue to be angry and upset or he could calm down and sign the papers authorizing the doctor to operate on my grandfather. Finally my father signed the papers.

I was back in my apartment, again asleep, when the phone rang the next morning. It was my grandmother. "Carey," she said, "he's gone." That's all she said. Then I heard her crying. Later my father told me that the operation had gone well. But my grandfather had been too weak. He never came out of the anesthesia. We buried him a few days later and my father returned to California.

A few days after my grandfather died Professor Short caught up with me after class and asked if the horse trainer whose obituary he had read in the *Times* was related to me. I said yes, he was my grandfather. Professor Short said that my grandfather sounded like a wonderful old gentleman and that he had never known anyone from the racetrack. I said yes, well, my father is also on the track and as a kid I used to spend a lot of time around the racetrack too. I looked around to see if anyone I knew saw me talking so intimately with Professor Short.

The professor asked if I'd like to have a cup of coffee with him. "Yes," I said. "Sure. Fine." Indeed, I would. The professor was nearly as famous as Lionel Trilling himself. His classes were among the most popular in the department. I could hardly believe my good fortune.

We went to a nearby café and talked about literature. I asked him about Norman Mailer, Philip Roth, and Saul Bellow. He asked me about the racetrack and whether I had any brothers and sisters and where I grew up. When a girl from his class came and sat in a booth near us, he bent forward and whispered to me that we should be careful what we said because she was a gossip. He said he wondered what she'd make of him having coffee with a "beautiful boy" like me. I thought that a funny thing for him to say but I didn't dwell on it.

Again after the next class we had coffee and talked about literature and Lionel Trilling and about me. And again after the next class.

After the fourth class the professor said, "Look, I live at the Blake Hotel. I'm going to go back for a swim and a drink. Why don't you come along?"

"Well," I said, "I don't know . . ."

"Oh, come on."

"Okay," I said.

It was a men-only pool. We swam naked. I began to feel a bit edgy splashing around with a naked professor and was glad when we got dressed and made our way to the hotel bar.

When our drinks came, I began telling the professor about Lisa and how crazy I was about her. He said it must be wonderful to be young now, able to live with our girlfriends. His generation had never known anything like that, he said. He asked me what I was going to do after Columbia and I said I didn't know yet, that I had earned a commission in the Marine Corps but that I had very mixed feelings about the military. I said I'd been thinking a lot lately about not accepting my commission. I explained how I could turn it down and complete the rest of my obligation in the reserves. The professor said he couldn't understand why I'd want to throw away three years in the service, especially as an officer. He said all his friends who had gone into the service in World War II had had nothing but contempt for officers.

"Look, I've got a bottle up in the room," the professor said when we had finished our second drink. "It'd be a lot cheaper to go upstairs and drink."

I said no, I didn't think so, I had to get back; I had work to do.

"What's the matter?" he asked. "Are you afraid of me?"

"Of course not," I said.

"Well, then," he said, "let's go up for just one drink."

"Well," I said, "all right."

I don't know how many drinks we had before I at last realized what I should have known at once. I felt angry, humiliated, sympathetic, and frightened all at once.

"Listen," I said. "I think there's been a misunderstanding."

The professor was incredulous. How could I think such a thing? Oh, no, he said, I had him all wrong.

Was it possible I had jumped to the wrong conclusion? I didn't think so. But if I had, I would feel terrible. I agreed to have one more scotch.

Then there was no doubt. He was explicit.

I got up to go.

"No," he said. "I was just teasing. I was just testing you. Don't be ridiculous. I'm a married man."

"Listen," I said. "I've really enjoyed getting to know you. I think you're a terrific teacher. I don't care if you're homosexual or not but . . . ."

The word seemed to excite him. He begged me to go to bed with him. He began to describe what he'd like to do with me.

As I walked quickly down the hall to the stairs, I heard him behind me. "No, no," he was saying, "I was just kidding. It's all a mistake. Come back. Come back."

I half-walked, half-ran the twenty blocks back to my apartment, feeling a wooziness that had little to do with all the alcohol I had consumed. When I reached the door to my apartment, I was drenched in sweat.

Two days later I got a postcard from him. On the face of the card was a picture of the hotel. The professor had drawn a stick figure lying on the street in front of the hotel. A dotted line led from one of the rooms to the stick figure in the street. On the other side were the words "The way I feel."

That week I decided to accept my Marine Corps commission.

One afternoon in the last week of February 1963, I dropped by the registrar's office and picked up my diploma. I was a college graduate. Okay, I said to myself, now what? Because the next Basic School class did not begin until May I faced the problem of what to do in the meantime. The Columbia University placement office put me in touch with a fat Long Island lawyer who ran an income-tax preparation business a couple of months out of the year. He had a number of outlets in various stores in Harlem. There was a spot open, he told me, at the Janal Drugstore at 125th Street and Lenox Avenue, virtually the crossroads of Harlem.

"But I don't know anything about income tax," I said.

"Don't worry about that," he said. "I'll teach you everything you need to know." The next Saturday I took a train to his office to learn the basics of income-tax law.

"Okay," the lawyer was saying. "Then you ask if he smokes. If he says yes, you ask how many packs a day. The tax on cigarettes works out to about twenty-two dollars a year for one pack a day. Okay, then you ask if he drives a car . . ."

A week later I found myself sitting on a stool behind the cosmetics counter at the Janal Drugstore. On the counter, with an arrow pointing to me, was a sign that read: "Federal Income Tax Expert." In front of me was a metal box containing nearly a thousand three-by-five cards. Each card represented a customer. It contained the person's name and address, the years "we" had prepared his tax forms, and, most important, how much we had last charged him. The standard rate was five dollars for a federal return and three dollars for the state, what the fat lawyer called "your basic eight-dollar package." Once a customer had come to us for two years without an increase I was supposed to charge him an extra dollar for each return. Customers who had been coming a decade were being charged up to twenty dollars for the "basic package." Their loyalty was costing them.

To many of the drugstore's customers, I appeared as a representative of officialdom. As a result, I was besieged with every kind of importuning; I listened to a hundred tales and problems with "the welfare," "the telephone," "the dope," "the numbers," "the doctor." Never mind that I barely knew the rudiments of income tax; to many I was "the Man."

As I sat there, day after day, witnessing a parade of poverty and intimidation, and only occasionally of triumphs great or small, I began to realize for the first time what it meant to be black in America. I also began to understand the human dimensions of what until then had just been another abstraction to me: "the civil rights movement." And, with the help of some of my customers, I was alerted to my own unconscious racism.

One afternoon an elderly, gray-haired woman handed me her W-2 forms. I saw that she worked in a laundromat. Her name was Bessie Williams.

"Well, Bessie," I said, "did you work anywhere else?"

The woman snatched the forms from my hand.

"You listen to me, white boy," she said. "My name is *Mrs*. Williams. Who do you think you are?" With that, she turned and walked out of the drugstore.

That night, walking back along 125th Street to my apartment, I stopped in a bar called the Top Hat. I ordered a scotch. I sipped it slowly, thinking about the woman who had walked out on me that afternoon. I began looking at the other customers, men mostly, trying to figure out what I saw and what I felt when I looked at them.

"What you staring at, white boy?"

My head jerked back and I felt my cheeks go flush. "Nothing," I said. "I'm . . . I'm sorry."

"Pay him no mind," I heard the man's companion say. "He probably never saw a black man before."

I looked at the second man. He was a big man with a magnificent head. He wore a beard.

"No," I said to him, "that's not it at all. I was just thinking about something. I didn't mean to stare."

We got to talking. The big man's name was Thomas Jefferson.

"But they call me Time," he said.

"What they really call him," said the second man, "is *Big Time*."

The two men bought me a drink. I bought them a drink. I told them about college and about my work at the Janal Drugstore. I asked Time what *he* did.

"This and that," he said.

We talked some more and I said I had to be going. Time shrugged his shoulders. I said I'd like to see him again, that I'd like to talk to him some more. He said he wasn't going anywhere. I could usually find him at the Top Hat.

I found him there the next night and the night after that. We talked about black people and white people and what he called the coming revolution. As Time got to know me better and began to trust me, he talked more and more about his hatred for white people. He was not a disciple of Elijah Muhammad, he said, but he did read the Muslim newspaper *Muhammad Speaks*. He said it told the truth about white people, that white people were "devils," and that it was white people who were violent, who were the enemy. I found it frightening but also strangely flattering to be told such things.

One night after work Time and I went together to see comedian Dick Gregory on stage at the Apollo Theater. After the show, we went backstage. We told Gregory that we'd liked his act and that we were going over to the Top Hat. If he'd like to come over, we'd like to see him and buy him a drink. He said sure, he'd drop by.

Then I did a strange thing: I called Professor Short. I hadn't spoken to him since that awful night months before. Although I didn't want to see Professor Short alone, I wanted him to know I bore no grudge for what had happened.

"Listen," I said when he answered his phone, "Dick Gregory's coming over to the Top Hat, this bar in Harlem, to talk with me and some friends. Why don't you come too?"

There was a pause on the telephone as he digested that piece of information.

"What's the address?" he said finally.

About eight of us in all, counting a couple of friends of Dick Gregory's and a couple of friends of Time's, eventually were gathered round a big table in a back room at the Top Hat. I loved the incongruity of Professor Short and Time and Dick Gregory arguing at the same table.

Dick Gregory said that whites were all racists and that blacks were perfectly justified in extracting "revenge" for "four hundred years of lynching niggers." It got pretty heated and we all had plenty to drink.

About two in the morning, when we were all too loud and too drunk, Professor Short said he was sorry but he had to go. A little later I suggested to Gregory that we all ought to adjourn, perhaps to continue when we were all more sober; perhaps he'd like to get together later in the week for lunch.

Gregory said, "Lunch, shit." He said the only reason I

wanted to have lunch with him was because he was Dick Gregory and I was a "celebrity fucker."

"I bet you'd never ask *him* to lunch," he said, cocking his thumb toward Time.

Time threw back his head and laughed. For the first time all evening Gregory was silent.

"What's so funny?" he asked finally.

Time told him that he'd had lunch at my apartment the day before.

We staggered out of the Top Hat about four in the morning. Gregory shook my hand and called me an okay dude. A couple of days later I got a note from Professor Short thanking me for having invited him. "Hope the Muslims didn't get you," he wrote at the end.

It was just after my income-tax stint that I got a call from a retired chief of detectives in the New York City Police Department. He had gotten to know my father in California by helping out around the stable walking "hots"—cooling out horses.

He wanted to meet me, wanted to buy me a dinner. What's more, he wanted a friend to meet me. The friend was a New York City detective. But in 1943 the friend had been my father's best buddy at boot camp in Parris Island.

I tried to put him off; time was running out before I was to report to Basic School and I wanted to spend every possible moment with Lisa. But, finally, I said okay.

The retired chief of detectives picked me up in his car. As soon as I had been introduced to his friend, the friend began to cry. His daughter, he said through sobs, had decided to become a nun.

Every few blocks on the way to the restaurant the detective would ask the retired chief of detectives to stop the car. He would disappear into a bar for a few minutes, then return to cry and to tell us again that his daughter was entering a nunnery.

By the time we arrived at the restaurant, a quiet place

where violinists strolled from table to table, the detective was quite drunk. He had never been in such a restaurant, he said, in "all his born days."

We had just been seated when the detective, with great fanfare, summoned the violinists. He spoke so loudly that every head turned toward our table. He told the musicians that he had never seen such a wonderful restaurant, that his daughter was entering a nunnery, and that this fine, fine boy right here beside him was soon going off to serve his country in the "fightin'est force the world has ever known." He said he had a very special request for the violinists. He would like very, very much for them to play a tune especially for this fine young man here at the table. Would they please play the Marine Corps Hymn?

In halting English the leader of the group said he was terribly sorry but he was not familiar with that particular selection. The detective looked at the musician disbelievingly, up and down, as if searching for some physical evidence of the turpitude implicit in such a confession. Finally he commanded them to listen; he was certain they could follow along. Then, to my mortification, the drunken detective began, in full voice, to sing "From the halls of Montezuma . . . To the shores of Tripoli . . ." Shortly, the violinists did their best to join in, though the Marine Corps Hymn and the violin are not entirely compatible.

A few mornings later I got out of a warm bed full of Lisa to serve God and country in the United States Marines.

July 28, 1963

Dear Lisa,

   It is another Sunday night at Basic School, and I am back, depressed as usual—but unusually depressed—more from the weekend itself than from the prospect of another week with three problems that will keep us out most of three nights.

I spent the weekend with my father. From the moment we met ("I had hoped you would be in uniform") we were at each other. He was at me, picking, picking, and I was so terribly uncomfortable. Everything I said he contradicted; at everything he said I nodded.

We talked *at* each other—he of his family, me of the Marine Corps—not understanding each other or caring, talking on completely different planes. If he made a joke I took it seriously, and vice versa.

Had you known, you could have seen us on television. My father ran a horse in a stakes race at Monmouth Park, and he was interviewed before the race. Near the end of the interview the announcer grabbed me and pointed to the cameras. I mumbled something stupid, really inane, about how I hoped we'd win and what a beautiful day it was. What an ass. Anyway, we won the race. I made a bet of $1,000 for the horse's owner and cashed it in for $2,900, which I passed on to him. My father made a bet of twenty dollars on a horse he used to train and lost it, and although he mentioned my birthday he didn't offer a cent. In fact, he even borrowed a dollar, or I guess I gave it to him.

Saturday night we went to a big charity ball at the track. He allowed me to have one drink ("You can do your drinking on your own," he said, "but not with me"), intimating either that I'm an alcoholic or that two drinks would have me screaming on the table.

I ran into Mike Mayfield at this ball and found myself trying to defend the Marine Corps—what a joke!—while he chortled and laughed his gassy laugh. But I liked him and wish now I could see some of the others on whom I turned my back at Columbia. Mike is not going back this year. Garrick lost his scholarship and together they are going to tour the West, earning their bread by the sweat of their brow, or something romantic like that.

Mike mentioned to his date that my girl, Lisa, was the sweetest-looking and sweetest girl in the world. I liked him for that.

Oh, honey, I'm so lonely. We all are I know, but

knowing it doesn't make it any easier. I wanted so much to have my father ease my loneliness but he just made me scared to be alive, afraid of doing something wrong. God, I feel so fucked up tonight!

And this weekend has shown me something else: I am never going to be a writer. I guess I've known it for some time but never admitted it. It never came out and announced itself as it did this weekend. Simon wrote a short story that was printed in a thing like the *Columbia Review* and was very good. All I ever do is talk about writing. I never write anything. I *can't* write anything. And then Mike Mayfield was going on about what a great writer I am and how I should be writing now, and there I was trying to explain that there wasn't time, there wasn't this or that. And suddenly it just walked up and said out loud that there never will be time or whatever it is I'm supposed to need. There just never will.

Oh, shit, I need you. I need you to be here to love me and to go for a walk and to talk about things. I want us to say quietly to each other that we love and need each other. This half of us sure does. I wish I could be with you and talk to you in person. But I'll call you Thursday at nine. I'll be staying here the next two weekends, I'm afraid, because of exams.

I feel better already, just having written to you. I hope you did well on your final. Are you still reading *Letting Go?* Judy gave me *Goodbye, Columbus,* his first. Pretty good so far, though more Jewish. Goodnight, darling. I love you very much.

What little enthusiasm we could muster for the six-month grind of Basic School was soon dissipated by the summer heat. In its place came a kind of mock bravado. As the days cooled and the first crisp winds moved in from off the sea, we turned restless, eager to put behind us a process we found increasingly pointless. "Spring butts"—the inevitable few lieutenants who rose at the end of each class to ask increasingly unnecessary questions about "tactical mount-out" or "summary courts-martial"—found themselves on the receiving end of an ever-louder chorus of booings. And each new administrative mixup, whether too few trucks to take us to a night field problem or a nonsensical last-minute change of equipment or schedule, brought forth three hundred voices raised in song: "Emm-eye-cee, kay-ee-why, emm-oh-you-ess-ee." Grown men, officers and gentlemen by definition, if not in fact, we had regressed into prepubescent childishness, fed by boredom and a growing anxiety about where we would be assigned and what we would be assigned to.

I wanted to go to Japan. I listed it as my first choice, followed by Okinawa. In an effort to protect myself against the terrible possibility of being sent to Camp Lejeune, North Carolina, home of the Second Marine Division, I had listed Camp Pendleton in California, home of the First, as my third and last choice for a duty station.

As for Military Occupational Specialties—my job—I had chosen intelligence first, artillery second (on the assumption that if I couldn't be an elite intelligence officer, I would at least get a platoon of my own). I rejected the infantry simply because its exhaustive promotion by everyone at Basic School made me suspicious. As my third choice I listed aviation supply, knowing that my only chance to get to Japan was with the air wing. Ideally I would be sent as an intelligence officer to Iwakuni, Japan, assigned to the First Marine Air Wing. Failing that, I would go—I thought—to Okinawa as an artillery officer. If, for some reason, I got neither my first nor my second choice in either category, I would then be sent to Iwakuni as an aviation supply officer.

I couldn't believe my orders. I couldn't believe, among the elated cries of my colleagues, what the unfeeling military bureaucracy had done to me. I stared at my MOS in disbelief. Three-oh, it read. Supply officer. Duty station: Cherry Point, North Carolina. Tropical Siberia with grits on the side: "Y'all come back and see us now." There was a saying in the Marine Corps that the reason Marine officers' wives were so dumb and ugly was because so many bachelor lieutenants were sent to North Carolina for their first tour of duty.

I sought out my platoon commander, Captain Farmer. For once he seemed subdued. Then he explained what had happened—why my preferences had been virtually ignored. Assignments were handed out on the basis of class standing, he said. In peer ratings—those given by my fellow lieutenants—I had done well, very well in fact. Academically, my grades were good. And, physically, I had done all I was supposed to do. "But," said Captain Farmer, "I personally rated you very low; in fact, among the lowest in the platoon."

"But sir," I said, unbelieving. "But why?"

"Attitude, lieutenant," he said.

"Attitude, attitude. Sir, what's wrong with my attitude?"

He opened a drawer in his desk and fished around in it. Finally he pulled out a packet of paper that I recognized as the latest version of the one-thousand-word autobiography that the Marine Corps never seemed to tire of asking us to write. He turned to a marked page in the middle. "My feelings about the Marine Corps," he read, "are, I must say, very ambivalent." He stopped to make a joke. "I had to look up 'ambivalent,'" he said. I smiled, nervously, as he continued. "Ever since I was very young, the Marine Corps held a special place in my imaginings. No doubt, my father's World War II service was largely responsible. I came out of a military school convinced that I wanted to be an officer, and that I wanted to be an officer in the most challenging branch. Thus I chose the Marines. My ambivalence arises out of my feelings about war and its basic futility, and my feelings about killing a fellow human being. I do not know how those feelings would change in a combat situation, but I must say that I hope that I do not have to find out." He looked up.

"And that's why you rated me low," I said, "for saying honestly what my feelings are? All the work I've done here counted for nothing because of one honest paragraph."

"Lieutenant," he said. "This isn't college. This isn't a creative writing class. This is the United States Marine Corps. Our job is war, our job is killing. As a platoon commander, you may have the lives of sixty or eighty or a hundred and twenty men depending on you and on your judgment. They want courage, they want direction, they want leadership. They don't want your 'ambivalence.' Lieutenant, you're goddam lucky you're still in uniform. That'll be all."

"Yes, sir," I said.

Once again I found myself amazed at the recuperative powers of the human psyche. Almost immediately my mind began to reinterpret the harsh facts of what appeared to be three years in Southern exile. At least it's the air wing, I rationalized. I'll be able to get weekend hops anywhere I want to go. New York every weekend if I want to. With Lisa.

Lisa. Scarcely an hour passed that I did not tune my thoughts to her, reassuring myself that, Cherry Point or no Cherry Point, somebody cared for me, missed me, and didn't care in the least how many pushups I could do, or how well I read maps, or how interesting I did not find mortars.

Her letters gave me reason to sit in a quiet room (when I could find one) and put my thoughts on paper. Somehow the arranging of them, the listing of them, the organizing of them, helped make sense of them.

Suddenly, with less than a month to go before graduation from Basic School, she stopped writing to me.

When a week passed without a letter, I telephoned her. No answer. I called again, later. Again no answer. The next day her roommate answered. "Lisa?" she asked. "Uh, Lisa's not here just now."

"Do you expect her?"

"Uh, yes. I . . . I think she'll be back this afternoon."

"Tell her I called. Tell her to call me."

But she didn't call. Not that day. Not the next. Again I tried to reach her. Again there was no answer. It was an old wound; I passed quickly from concern through suspicion to something approaching frenzy. By Wednesday I could think of little else. One minute I'd almost convince myself that there were any number of reasonable explanations. Midterms. A letter got lost. Her parents were sick. A paper to write. The next minute I didn't believe any of it.

One day, nearly ten days after I had last heard from her, the day's schedule presented me with a rare opportunity. I searched out a friend at lunch. "There's only one class this afternoon," I said to him. "They'll only take the roll one time."

His eyes widened.

"Yeah," I said. "I want to go to New York."

He didn't want me to go. It wasn't just that he would have to be the one to call out "Here" when my name was called. He was worried for me.

"It's AWOL, you know," he told me.

"That's how much you know about military law," I answered, cockier than I felt. "It's UA, unauthorized absence."

The attempt at humor worked.

"Okay," he said. "It's your ass. Good luck."

I left right after lunch—about one o'clock—driving my Volkswagen at a steady seventy, stopping only once for gas and a sandwich on the New Jersey Turnpike. I drove hunched over the wheel, excited by the risk I was taking, anxious about what awaited me in New York. I felt very alive, much as I had those nights a year before sneaking into Hewitt Hall.

It was after five when I turned off Riverside Drive at 116th Street. Miraculously I found a parking place. I locked the car and ran across the street, my hands sweating, to the old, ugly apartment house that had been taken over by Barnard some months before and converted into the dorm where Lisa now lived.

I raced through the lobby to the elevator, almost overcome by the familiar stench of dead rats, live cats, and urine. The elevator was slow, its operator as decrepit as the surroundings. Finally I reached the ninth floor. I knocked on the door to the apartment Lisa shared with two other girls.

"I'm looking for Lisa," I said.

"She's not here." The voice was familiar from the telephone. It was still full of hesitation and hiding.

I pushed by the girl, not without thinking of the many bad movies I'd seen where overanxious young men push by protective secretaries to confront the boss in person.

I opened the door to Lisa's room, not knowing what I'd find.

It was empty, the bed made, cigarettes in ashtrays. It smelled of Lisa. The closet, open, reassured me with its rows of familiar clothes and shoes. Suddenly I felt foolish, childish, overdramatic. Books, opened and unopened, gathered dust on tables. The radio I had given her sat smugly on a small table by her bed.

I felt tricked by my own imaginings, as if I had tried to turn a conventional life and a conventional girlfriend into the stuff of high drama. Or, more like it, melodrama.

I sat down and took a cigarette from a pack on her desk. Near the pack I saw a letter from me. I started to pick it up, to read it. Then I saw other letters. They were not from me, but the handwriting was familiar. It was Porter's.

What? I thought. Porter writing to Lisa? Whatever for? What about?

"Darling," it began, and something in my stomach seemed to explode, sending flashes through my body. The jolt of it knocked the wind out of me. My eyes raced over the page, gulping in whole paragraphs: "I don't care any more. You must tell Carey. . . . Don't you understand that our love is the most important thing in the world? . . . I think back on those nights this summer. . . . We will spend our lives together."

For a second I couldn't move. My arms and legs felt no longer attached to my body. Then they began to move, my right arm reaching across the desk, knocking everything to the floor in one motion. Now I was standing up and the books and the ashtrays and the radio were careening across the room, crashing on top of each other. I ripped the covers from the bed, then turned the bed itself over. I kicked the desk, and tore at Porter's letter. I threw the lamp at the wall where it exploded into pieces. Only gradually did I become aware of people at the door, their mouths and eyes open, staring silently. I pushed past them, down the corridor, taking the stairs three at a time. (And yet I felt as if I were moving soundlessly in slow motion.) I had to get out. Had to move. Had to begin to burn up the jolts of adrenalin and energy whipping through my body. I had to find Lisa, and at the same time I knew I would. I knew, or thought I knew, that my actions were no longer under my control, that somehow it had all been scripted.

That was why I wasn't the least surprised when I saw her coming toward me through the front-entrance revolving door. Her eyes said she knew that I knew. She backed away from me, holding her books as a shield against me. I grabbed for the lapel of her coat and, clutching it, swung with an open hand across her face, catching her hard on the cheek and knocking her down.

"You whore! You bitch!" I screamed at her. Tears suddenly poured from my eyes. She was crying too. When she got up I swung again, ineffectually, intending to miss, and stumbled out into the night.

She followed me. She came to me and put her arms around me. We stood together crying, our arms around each other until we ran out of tears.

Later we talked, sitting in the parked Volkswagen. She tried to explain. I tried to understand. Neither of us succeeded. She said that when I went away she had thought it only a matter of time for us, that both of us were only acting out a part in a play we both knew was closing.

We went to a little bar, a favorite hangout of ours, and drank too much beer. The beer confused me. I had been betrayed. I wanted to be hard, cold, and unforgiving. Instead I began to want her as I had never wanted anyone. I told myself no. I must leave her and never see her again. But after the next beer I was thinking that the best justice would be to make love to her and *then* never see her again. And after the next beer I was certain of it.

We went back to her apartment and fucked each other angrily. The next thing I knew it was two o'clock in the morning, I felt worse than I had ever felt in my life, and I had four hours to drive to Quantico in time to make reveille and avoid a court-martial.

Three times I awoke to find myself on the shoulder of the parkway. But just at six o'clock I pulled into the Basic School parking lot. I sneaked into the dorm, changed into my utilities, and fell out for formation.

I spent the day making plastic bombs and blowing up bunkers and fortifications.

November 3, 1963:

I feel at the low ebb of my life. I am withdrawn and solemn. I am dejected and uncommunicative. The love affair that absorbed me these past two years has dissolved, or rather exploded. I try to keep my mind on other things, but I cannot. I am bitter, full of hate and self-pity. I am at the end of a difficult summer and at the beginning of a cold winter. My sole wish is to forget and to find a new life.

I keep imagining Porter and Lisa together and it is like a spike driven into my bowels. Love and hate are inextricably bound; I do not know which is the stronger at the moment, nor do I see any solution that would alleviate either. A crime of passion is a consideration, but only for an instant. They are not worth the momentary gratification. Perhaps only time can ease the total nothingness I feel.

I suppose the only thing I could wish is for them both to beg separate and individual forgiveness, which I could never give. But the satisfaction would be sweet. I hope and pray that they never see each other again. I know this cannot be. Life is shitty, society savage, and man alone.

The next week, for reasons unclear to me, I sent Porter a picture of Lisa with a note that said I had received my orders. I told him I was being sent as part of an honor guard to Egypt at the Sphinx.

In the last few weeks of Basic School our officers pretty much gave up on us. They seemed as anxious as we were to have it over with. We were thoroughly salty by then—no less than if we had just stormed Corregidor—and openly contemptuous of the other companies coming along months behind us. A captain lectured us about a recoil-less rifle, referring to it repeatedly as "this little bear." When the inevitable "Any questions?" came, Lieutenant Whitman stood up. "Yes, sir," he said. "How much does that little bear weigh?"

At the end of a mortar demonstration we were asked by another captain to give the enlisted men a hand packing up the mortars. Where three months earlier we would have bellowed "Yes, sir!" in unison and raced from the stands to pack up the equipment, now we simply applauded.

I remember these little incidents, but I don't remember much about myself. I was numb. I felt my life in limbo.

There were letters to Lisa, letters from Lisa. Letters apologetic and contrite. We finally agreed that since I had no other place to go for my five-day leave at the end of Basic School, a time that we had planned for months to spend together, I might as well come ahead and stay in New York.

I'm sure there must have been some sort of graduation ceremony at Basic School and, with it, backslapping and well-wishing and congratulations. I don't remember any of it. I don't remember driving to New York. I don't remember my reunion—it must have been awkward—with Lisa. I only remember a morning, it may have been my first back in the city, it may have been my second.

It was a Friday. Lisa went off to class and I ran into an old acquaintance, a professional student who had been taking courses in various Columbia departments for years, a man full of so many dreams that he never seemed able to organize any to any purpose. He lived what he boasted was a happy life, reading and playing tennis (I had met him on the tennis court) and collecting wives (he was on his third), mistresses, and friends. He spotted me walking into a roach-infested coffee shop, a kind of unofficial way station where one was always insured of a decent English muffin and surly service.

He joined me for a coffee and then, with the charming cajolery that formed the major element of his appeal, insisted I go with him to his apartment to admire the products of his latest enthusiasms, painting and poetry.

Once there, he opened a gallon jug of white wine, something I rarely drank. I looked at his paintings, great swirls of abstract pastels—lemon-and-lime-flavored clouds—and listened to his poetry—euphoric odes to life in general and abundant sex in particular. And I drank his wine.

The more I drank, the more I came to see Marvin as he wanted to be seen: wise, mature, caring. With the wine came a new appreciation for this poet who listened so sympathetically to my tale of betrayal. And with more wine came the belief that if Marvin could only see it all, understand it all, he would be able to tell me what I must do. I decided he must come with me to lunch with Lisa. He agreed.

As Lisa dutifully prepared our meal I began drunkenly to disparage her, at first by innuendo, gradually more explicitly, for the benefit of my new-found savant. It was not an hour that I care to recall in very great detail. I may have called her "slut." I think the tone was more what-do-you-think-of-a-girl-like-this-who-would-do-such-a-thing-to-a-fellow-like-me? How easily we do elevate our righteousness!

But then it stopped. The radio music was suddenly, terribly, interrupted. "Dallas, Texas: The President of the United States has been shot."

Marvin and Lisa fell silent. "Oh, no," I moaned. "Oh, God, no! Oh, God, please let him be all right."

We sat and waited the torturous but still hopeful twenty-five minutes until the announcer said, "The President of the United States is dead."

And then I put my head in a pillow and began to cry. It was dark out by the time I woke up.

Lisa and I spent that weekend in front of a television set trying to sort out what had happened. The shooting of Lee Harvey Oswald by Jack Ruby shook loose my last vestige of faith in the nation's exalted destiny. Chaos and anarchy seemed rampant.

I wore my blue dress uniform for the first time in public on the day of national mourning. Lisa and I went to a memorial service at Riverside Church.

The next day I said good-by to her. I wasn't due in North Carolina for two more days, but there just didn't seem any point in hanging around. I drove to Baltimore and spent the night at McDonogh, my first visit back since graduation more than four years before.

As I headed south the next morning, I listened to Lyndon Johnson on the radio. He was delivering his first speech as President to a joint session of Congress. "All I have," he began, "I would have given gladly not to be standing here today. The greatest leader of our time has been struck down by the foulest deed of our time . . ."

The longer I listened to him, the more I felt I had unfairly judged him and the more he affected me.

I got lost in Washington, as I always do, but found myself at last—as if directed—in front of the Capitol building. I parked the car and put my head on my hands on the steering wheel, listening to Johnson. When he had finished speaking, I wiped my eyes dry and walked to a spot in front of the Capitol, joining a small group of people standing behind a line of limousines. From an entrance to the Capitol came the muffled applause of hands brought together very slowly, a sound unlike any I had ever heard. I saw the new President walk slowly to a waiting limousine, his hand raised in acknowledgment.

Two men approached me: Robert McNamara and Robert Kennedy. McNamara's eyes were red; tears streamed unashamedly from the brother's. The two of them got into a limousine and were driven away.

I drove to Arlington Cemetery. I walked up a hill to see the grave of the fallen President. I stood for a while, turned, and walked back down the hill. I looked back one last time, then started the car and headed for my new duty station.